WE ARE THEIR HEAVEN

ALSO BY ALLISON DUBOIS

Don't Kiss Them Goodbye

WE ARE THEIR HEAVEN

HEAVEN

Why the Dead Never Leave Us

ALLISON DUBOIS

SIMON &
SCHUSTER

London · New York · Sydney · Toronto

A CBS COMPANY

First published in Great Britain by Simon & Schuster UK Ltd, 2006
A CBS COMPANY

3 5 7 9 10 8 6 4 2

Simon & Schuster UK Ltd
Africa House
64–78 Kingsway
London WC2B 6AH

www.simonsays.co.uk

Simon & Schuster Australia
Sydney

A CIP catalogue record for this book is available from
the British Library.

ISBN 0-7432-9544-7
EAN 9780743295444

Designed by Sarah Maya Gubkin

Printed and bound in Great Britain by
The Bath Press, Bath

This book is dedicated to Joe, my fantastic husband, and my incredible little girls. They have made my life sweet and meaningful. Words can never express my gratitude for their love.

To those who live and those who live again. Especially, little Lindsey Whelchel who died young but touched many.

I also dedicate We Are Their Heaven *to some of the best mediums/friends to have ever lived. You have helped pave the way for those who will follow behind us and who will learn from us and hopefully exceed us.*

I would like to thank Laurie Campbell, who will never be surpassed as a medium or friend; George Dalzell, who has more energy and heart of most anyone I know; and Sally Owen, not only a great medium but a woman whose character can never be questioned—it's outstanding. We have all since left the lab, having contributed many years of our lives to science, and now we move forward helping clients and law enforcement to bring the change that we were born to bring.

Contents

FOREWORD

Joe DuBois

How Do I Know?

Even before Allison completed her first book, her mind was already working on this one. She already knew the title would be *We Are Their Heaven* and had a clear idea of what it would be about. She told me that people often ask her about heaven. I began thinking, What a great idea, I love heaven! I also enjoyed writing a chapter in her first book and hoped to be able to do it again, but who am I to write about heaven? I am not a heaven expert. I have not been there, but I hope to go (no time soon). I have only read one book on the topic, which is helpful but hardly exhaustive research.

I am an expert at some things. I do know my wife, Allison. She *is* an expert on what happens after we die. That may seem like a bold statement, but it is one I am confident in making. I have known this wonderful woman for thirteen years. I know her daily life. I have seen her at her strongest, when her guard is up and she is ready to take on the world. I have seen her win a war of words with radio interviewers who are more interested in their own agenda than in getting to know Allison or learning about life after death. I have seen her in her most vulnerable state, when her guard is down and she is loving her family as a mother and a wife. At these times, her heart is open to us and she lets me in. It is an amazing privilege to go there with her. If I need to be clearer, I love my wife and I am very proud of her.

I also know a thing or two about aerospace engineering, aka "rocket science." Much debate can be held over a cold beer as to who is permitted to don the moniker "rocket scientist," and I am actually a little embarrassed when people call me this. I am embarrassed because I would reserve the title for heroes of mine like Robert Goddard or Wernher von Braun, who were both geniuses in the development of modern rocketry. Allison quickly reminds me that I have spent my career in aerospace on projects including experimental satellites, jet engine valves, and yes, as a matter of fact, rocket engine valve performance analysis and control system design.

At this point you are asking yourself, "If this is a book about heaven, why is he writing about himself?" I am writing about myself because I want to establish that I am a critical thinker. When I am confronted with an anomalous situation,

I do not immediately jump to any conclusion. I try to thoughtfully and rationally come to terms with the very interesting things that happen around my house. I now tell you what I have learned about Allison and what she does as a medium so that you may hear her message and take it to heart.

Allison's mediumship ability is a natural talent, a gift, some would say. She did not go to school to develop her abilities. However, she has spent a life honing her skills by practicing and not accepting mediocrity. Her talent is not different from what many people experience on a daily basis. Hers is just clearer and more obvious.

Since she has had this ability her entire life, she has known that a person's consciousness, whatever that may be, survives the death of the body. This has profoundly shaped who Allison is. Whereas most of us have to rely on belief and faith to comprehend heaven, Allison has to deal with it in a more visual sense.

Allison grew up knowing that when people die, they remain closely connected with the people left behind. They are close, yet they might as well be a million miles away because they can rarely be seen or heard by their living loved one. She was taught as a child to believe in an ethereal heaven that was described in an abstract way and involved many rules for proper entry, yet she plainly saw people who had died all around her. Being put in a situation where she saw one thing and was taught something slightly different would prove to be very frustrating. Thankfully, Allison worked through it and developed a very strong sense of self and the ability to be strong in her convictions. Allison sees the world in black and white with no gray. Allison does not live by rules, she lives by what she feels is right and is guided by her heart.

Allison and I have had the "why me" conversation several times. This is the conversation where she questions why she has her gift. The most recent time was this past summer. It was a family Sunday. We went swimming with our children, then followed up with a delicious barbecue. In typical American fashion, I grilled the hamburgers and Allison made a nice macaroni salad. I have a great secret hamburger recipe that Allison loves. I suggest that every dad should have one, even if it is just adding a little teriyaki sauce to the beef. Mine is more complicated and does not involve teriyaki, but it lets my kids know that I love them because I take extra time to make the meal just the way they like it. Fallon often helps me make the burgers. One time she snuck a pinch of sugar into the sauce. I did not tell anyone, and everyone loved the burgers that night. Now she is in charge of her own special secret ingredient. Please don't tell her that I shared her secret ingredient.

After this wonderful day, our children decided to go inside to play, and Allison and I remained on the patio to enjoy a glass of wine. This is when the "why me" conversation started. This question was asked not in a woeful way but more as part of a search for purpose. In Allison's life, she searches for the purpose of events. I, on the other hand, am more content to believe that some things just are the way they are without greater purpose. Time and time again, Allison will point out how a series of seemingly random and unconnected events, when taken as a whole, show a bigger plan.

I reminded Allison of what makes her so special besides the fact that she is a medium. She is also very intelligent, beautiful, strong-willed, honest, charitable, wise, and young at heart, and she has integrity. To put it simply, Allison is the best person I know. Allison is a handshake kind of person. If she makes a promise, she will keep it. She likes to play it off that she somehow has cowboy blood in her. She was raised in Phoenix and the older Phoenicians were straight shooters, but I believe Allison would have been this way regardless of where she was born. Allison is who she is because she is who she is!

To explain this seemingly ridiculous sentence, I must share a brief story about Allison when she was visiting Hawaii as a teenager. Through a series of choices made by the then sixteen-year-old Allison, she found herself on a surfboard far from the beach being circled by a large shark. At that point, she told God that if he kept her safe, she would do whatever he asked and that she would "help people." God sent a current to carry her safely to shore. He kept his side of the deal, now she is keeping hers. The first "she is who she is" means that she is doing what God has asked of her; the second part, "because she is who she is," means that she knows no other way than to have integrity in her word. Allison is the only person I know who argues with God. This does not mean that she is irreverent. It means that God is always in Allison's life. She talks (prays) to God and listens to God. She has never told me that God speaks to her directly, but she describes his indirect acknowledgment and guidance. Since she is honest, she will let God know if she is unhappy about what is being asked of her. It was a little unnerving at first, but I have gotten used to it. This is a lesson that I am learning from Allison: be honest with yourself and live knowing that you are bare in front of God.

I know that my dad shares in my life today, even though he passed away over thirteen years ago. Allison has talked to my dad for me on many occasions. What I really mean is that Allison will listen to my dad and tell me what he says. She's my interpreter. I know that he can hear me, and now I recognize that the little feeling I get sometimes that he is around is right. Now that I have acknowledged that he is around, I don't need to have Allison tell me quite so much.

My dad does not always talk in subtle ways. He has had the opportunity to mysteriously set off fire alarms. Without a doubt the most amazing sign that he was near was that Fallon was born on the fifth anniversary of his death in the same hospital where he died. The hospital was not the closest one to our house, but Allison thought the nurses were nicer there. At the time, I thought my dad had died April 28, but it turned out that he had died April 29. My mom informed me that he had died after midnight in the middle of the night. I didn't learn this until we had Fallon, and it made her birth even more special.

I also know when my father-in-law is around. He was quite a man and I love him very much. He has an incredible way of playing just the right song on the radio, right when you need it. He also has the knack of making Allison happy. I just wish I could hear him better when I am picking out anniversary presents. I am sure if I could hear him right now, he would be saying, "Don't listen to me, listen to your wife. She will tell you what makes her happy."

I have learned by being married to Allison that we are here on this earth to live and love one another. I have learned why it is so important to be yourself, to be honest, and to have integrity. I have learned that my father, grandparents, and ancestors are here with me because they love me. They could be off doing other things, but they choose to visit me instead. As Allison says, "We are their heaven." The journey of writing this chapter has helped me to realize that I do know what heaven is. Allison is my heaven.

INTRODUCTION

While writing this book, I decided that giving my perspective is good, but giving my perspective and the perspective of the person whom I read will be more beneficial to my readers. I think it's important for people who are grieving to have others to relate to, people who walk their same path. In this book, the people whom I've read speak in their own words about how they moved forward and what our meeting did for them. I share details about the process of each reading. I also illustrate why being a medium has such a great impact on my life, as well as the lives of my family.

I met a lot of new people through the media tour for my first book, during radio and television interviews and question-and-answer sessions before book signings. I noticed there are common threads of questions. Many people ask what heaven is like. There is an obvious concern around what happens to our deceased loved ones. People wonder about the connection of the dead to the living. I often get questions from people who are concerned that their mourning a loved one is preventing the loved one from fully passing over to the other side.

This book addresses some of the various ways in which people die, for example by suicide or accident, and the different ways in which they show us that they remain. A question that I hear often is, Why do the deceased want to remain after death? Well, of course because they love us, but there are other reasons as well. Our deceased relatives want to connect with the living because our lives are based on emotion and continuing to learn and grow, as are their own. They willingly stay with us to share in our emotion and to help teach us what we need to learn. Often they want to make sure that we don't repeat their mistakes, the things they ended up regretting and would do differently if they had the chance. It also brings them a great deal of joy to share in our lives, especially when we're talking about them or to them. It's important to stay open to the messages that are sent from those who go before us, those who are still a part of us. Part of my book's purpose is to open the living up to the spirits who continue to share in their loved ones' lives. Loving people who have died doesn't hold them here, as some think. It gives them life. They stay around us because we are what they consider utopia, their "heaven."

There is a heaven, a flawless place where we exist after we die. There are white skies and blue water that the eyes of the living cannot see. There are children running through perfect blades of brilliant emerald grass with sunshine bouncing off every strand of their hair. There are old men fishing on the same banks that they fished from when they were boys, with the puppy that died when they were small. Couples who were married for fifty years now look like they did when they were first married, as they stroll hand in hand down a path by a tree. It's all that and more.

Yet even with all that, it's not entirely heaven to those who've died because, usually, not all their loved ones are there. Try to understand: it's the flaws of the living, our attempts to figure out who we are, how to connect with others, and how to spend our time on earth that interests those who've passed. They want to see how our character stands up when we're challenged. They want to see their namesakes move through life. They want to see children born and anniversaries celebrated, help the sick get better, lend strength to us in times of weakness. Parents who die still want to be there for their kids on the days they're needed most. Children who die want to see their parents, siblings, and friends laugh again and, most important, "feel" their presence and continuing love. So, yes, they have a beautiful sanctuary where everything is as it should be, but never forget that *we* are their heaven.

CHAPTER I

Here Again

The loss of a child has to be the hardest loss to endure. I have three daughters who mean the world to me, and I know that every parent's biggest fear is to outlive his or her child. There is not a day that goes by that I don't thank God for my kids, and I know for parents whose children have died, they thank God for every day that they had with their child. I hope my readers will find some comfort and inspiration in the stories shared in this chapter. The connection between parent and child can never be broken, not even by death. Our children are a part of us not just physically but spiritually as well. Parents are the caretakers, the protectors of a helpless little life that grows under our love and guidance. I believe that is why there is a certain amount of guilt that follows the loss of a child, more so than with other losses. Love is indivisible, so there can never really be a good-bye, only "Till we meet again."

I asked a woman whom I read to detail the loss of her daughter and her experience with me. I also have included how I was impacted by the reading personally.

A MOTHER'S LOVE

Oddly enough, the first time I "met" Allison DuBois was in the spring of 2005. However, my very first contact with her was the sound of a soft-spoken, sweet voice with a western drawl coming to me over two thousand miles of phone lines connecting me in New York to Allison in Arizona. What I was not prepared for that day was that we would have a party line connection!

Looking back, I see that the events leading up to this meeting were like the perfect choreography of a professional dance ensemble. My daughter Candace died at the age of fifteen, in September of 2002, in an automobile accident while riding with her brother in his car. The accident left our son in a coma for several days. We began to experience signs of our daughter's presence from the day of her funeral, first through close friends, and then personally. It was clear to me she was around, and that gave me the strength to get up every day. But my husband could not grasp the concept of a world beyond this physical one. His pain and his doubt were unshakable and even made me question my own convictions.

Meanwhile, lightbulbs went out in our home, only to turn back on as we stood there with a replacement bulb in our hands. Electronic sounds emanated from our bedroom thermostat. It seemed the electrician, at my husband's request, was suddenly spending way too much time at our house.

By now, we had finished reading books on grief and had both concluded that they offered little help. We moved into religious books for an explanation of why such a wonderfully bright, vivacious, and talented young child could be taken from this world. Where was the justice? Weren't we taught that God was all-loving? When you lose a child, it is hard to understand why the child had to go. Questioning God seems to make sense.

And then one day, while waiting for a conference with our son Jon's rehabilitation team, we stopped at a nearby bookstore for a cup of coffee. And there on a display, just a few feet from our table, was a book that included accounts of mediums being studied in a university laboratory. Of course we bought it, along with a few other books. We wanted to explore spirituality and look outside the box.

A few days later, I experienced the most unbelievable sign from the other side . . . except this time it wasn't from my daughter. I was on my way to pick up Jon from a physical therapy session when I suddenly had to stop driving, as

I became overwhelmed with the gnawing need to know the age of a little girl who had lost her life days after being crushed by a gym door in a nearby elementary school in 1991. I didn't know why, I just felt compelled to find out. Once composed, I got back on the road and continued on to pick up my son. Upon our arrival home, we were greeted by my husband, Tom, who had just located a meeting of The Compassionate Friends (a grief support group for anyone who's had a loss), and we needed to eat our dinner quickly in order to arrive on time. (Newcomers were asked to arrive early to chat with "buddies" before the meeting got started.) On the way there, I shared with Tom the strange experience of the day.

The meeting ritual at this chapter of The Compassionate Friends was to go around the room so that each person would have the opportunity to speak about who they were and whom they had lost. The woman seated behind me took her turn; as she introduced herself to the group, I recognized her as the mother of the little girl who had "visited" me earlier in my car. I had had this awesome interaction with this other mother's deceased child. It was as if I was being prepped to see my own daughter. I dug my nails into my husband's arm as I took in the enormity of the moment.

When we broke for coffee, I went to talk with her and I told her of the "coincidence" earlier in the day. "How nice," she replied. "Today is my daughter's birthday. She would have been twenty-one years old."

Well, Tom and I have been married for more than thirty

years. He had never known me to lie or even bend the truth, but had I not shared the story with him on the way to The Compassionate Friends meeting, he never could have truly appreciated the experience of a spirit child's finding a way to let her mom know that she was there with her on this very special birthday.

By this time, my husband had finished reading the book on mediumship testing and had decided to contact the university mentioned in the book. Our goal was to have a personal reading with each one of the mediums who had taken part in the experiments in the book. If he could find a scientific explanation for the little girl's "visit," then we might also have a method by which to reach our daughter.

In February 2003, we received a response from a scientist at the university. In March 2003, we had a phone conversation with our first research medium, Laurie Campbell. Later, in August, we flew to Arizona to meet with Laurie and to participate in an experiment. It was all so wonderfully healing for me, but Tom, so grounded in the physical world, wanted still more proof!

Eventually I received a call from the laboratory at the university saying we were invited to participate in a large experiment that was about to begin. They didn't have to ask me twice. I was even ready to hop on a plane, until the coordinator explained it was all to take place over the phone!

A few weeks later, on a predetermined day, I sat home as instructed, awaiting the call from the scientist. Just the thought of connecting to my daughter again lifted me higher than I had felt since before her passing.

When the phone finally rang, the scientist explained that I could not say a word; as soon as she got the medium on the other line, we were to hang up! *Hang up?* Yes, this was one of many parts to the experiment. I would be called back again in half an hour. I held on as the scientist dialed another number to conference the call. The soft-spoken, sweet voice with a western drawl at the other end said, "Hello."

The scientist said, "Hi, Allison, are you ready? When we hang up, you are to begin part 1A," and then everyone hung up. Part 1A was where the medium gave her information on the deceased to the scientist. I sat there for a moment waiting for something special to happen to me—a special feeling, a sign, something to tell me that this other world was busy with the science of the afterlife, or at least that my daughter was nearby waiting her turn to speak.

By the time the phone rang again half an hour later, I was filled with anticipation. Allison was now introduced to me. I was introduced as the "sitter" to Allison and reminded that I was to remain silent. The discarnate (deceased) was introduced as the "daughter of the sitter."

I took nineteen pages of notes as Allison brought through facts about Candace as if my daughter were standing right in front of her! And perhaps she was. Allison mentioned a cat on the other side with Candace. She described some of her passing, my dad and how he passed, the sports that Candace enjoyed, her shyness before warming up to new people, how she always sat in the kitchen watching me cook chocolate pudding on the stove, how she loved to go to the movies. Allison relayed the message "I can take care of you now like you took care of me."

The messages came fast and furious. But one message in particular helped me with a feeling common among those who are grieving—guilt.

"The King and I," Allison said. "She says, 'Mom was watching.' "

I wanted to speak, but I bit my tongue.

As a mother of three, I literally lived in my car, driving from Little League to karate to birthday parties to school events. As the kids got involved in more and more activities, Tom and I had to start picking and choosing the events we could attend, and more often than not we would have to split up. Tom always opted to attend our daughter's events. The two of them always had a very special bond. But it was the presentation of *The King and I* at the elementary school that I and not my husband had attended. With her death, it haunted me that I had missed so many of her games and performances, and here was Allison showing me that Candace was pointing out the play that she had been so excited to be in and I had been so proud to attend.

We could have hung up then, and I would have been grateful, although I really wanted this reading to go on forever. The connections, no matter how frequent or significant, are never enough when you have lost a child.

Allison continued, as Candace talked about leaving behind her brother, "I miss him, and I'm still teasing him." She reported that she no longer had to eat the green vegetables I insisted be consumed with each dinner, and that she knew about the new puppy our cousin had just gotten.

The information continued to flow. Half of me wanted it to stop, so I could let Allison know just how significant these tidbits of information were; the other half wanted to sit and listen to Candace for eternity.

We had been on the phone for almost two hours now, completing parts 1b, 2b, and 2c of the experiment with a fifteen-minute break in between. Each part was different. In the first there was no living sitter present. Then a living sitter was on the phone to listen but not respond while a researcher asked the medium a series of questions. The process was in depth and very structured because it was a scientific experiment. We finally came to part 3, described in the labs instructions as "You and the medium will engage in a traditional reading in which you are no longer silent and an open dialogue can occur."

Yippee! I can talk. I was not interested in a "traditional reading." What I needed from this fabulous woman was to share with her some of the things that she was bringing through that told me in no uncertain terms that Candace had joined us on this party line. I was now formally introduced to Allison DuBois.

What I didn't expect at this point was that Candace had not hung up the phone. And so, as I attempted to chat with

Allison about *The King and I,* Candace was busy calling her brother "butthead." And as I mentioned the new toddler who had moved in next door with the unusual name of Cole (whom Allison had mentioned previously in the reading by name!), Candace also told us in all certainty that Cole knows she's there!

And I now could hear Allison weeping at the other end. "She loves you. She says you're a 'great mom,' and she felt very close to you. And she said, Dad, he hurts himself physically by keeping this all inside."

And then, just to make certain we all knew it was she, Candace threw us some of her teasing humor. Allison described my mother-in-law, focusing on the very thing that Candace had always teased Grandma about: she showed Allison a little woman with platinum hair and her eyebrows drawn on. My positive response to Allison, elicited one word from Candace. " 'Grammy!' " Allison told me. "She sends her love by name."

And then there was the picture that Allison had described early on in the experiment: "A picture of her with a best friend or sister . . . a female, just the two of them with their arms around each other, smiling towards the camera." Before I hung up, I wanted Allison to know that she had described the photo I looked at every day on my desk in my office. No sooner had the words left my mouth, when Allison said, "Happy Valentine's Day. She says to tell you, 'Happy Valentine's Day.' "

For a moment I was confused; February was months

away! Then I recalled that it had been Valentine's Day when the lab had finally responded to the many e-mails and letters that my husband had written. It was 4:30 p.m. when we said our thanks and our good-byes. I was now in a new place emotionally. It wasn't just because of Allison's ability to connect with dead people. It was because Allison had visited with Candace. She saw her. She spoke with her, and my little girl spoke back, telling her things only she and I knew, and then sending messages of love, guarantees that she was well, happy, and where she needed to be, promises to be there watching us, confirmation that she had been spending time with us, even sitting and having dinner with us. I couldn't wait to go over my notes with Tom.

The next morning, I awoke feeling different. Yes, I checked. The hole in my heart was still there, but it wasn't bleeding anymore. I dressed and went down to my office. There was the picture. Candace with her sister—her best friend, her confidante—dressed up, arms around each other and smiling into the camera, just as Allison (or was it Candace?) had described.

I lovingly removed the photo from its display, turning on my scanner so I could e-mail it to the laboratory to back up the data of the experiment. This is the science, I thought. This is what my husband needed, and this is what the lab must have to back up the data. I flipped the photo over.

And written on the back was "Valentine's Day Dance."

Looking back now, it seems that marked the moment when my life journey profoundly changed. Soon after that,

Tom had his first "visit" from Candace (feeling her presence and seeing her in a dream), and her sister experienced a "visit" on the same day. However, we all learned very quickly that we could not share this excitement with just anybody. Instead, we needed first to be certain that we were talking to "believers."

It wasn't long before we realized that we were not alone in either the experiences we were having or our fear of sharing them. Talking to others about seeing the deceased in dreams or feeling their presence around you, even seeing them before your eyes, is hard. You don't want to talk to nonbelievers and deal with their personal hang-ups about the afterlife and have their reaction somehow take away from your special experience.

Throughout my life, I have not been afraid of affecting change. It was clear to me that the Western way of thinking denied the existence of a powerful force—a force that many people report experiencing firsthand, a force that can provide wonderful healing to the bereaved—and that this mind-set clearly needs to change.

Bringing Candace Through

In 2003 I was set up for a mediumship test through a university. I was contacted via telephone by a scientist with a series of questions pertaining to a formal test. I was asked not only to answer questions but to provide the information that I received from the deceased. There were two different readings to be administered for two different people who had never met and had each experienced a loss.

For the first test, I kept seeing a young girl who showed herself playing volleyball. She also kept talking about *"The King and I"* and the "play," as she put it. I told the scientist that she'd either been in this play or somehow it was her favorite. The "sitter," who wasn't allowed to speak in the first phase of the test, was asked to hit a button on the phone to confirm that she felt all the information given was indeed that of the deceased she wished to contact. She did. After the initial phase, the sitter along with the scientist were permitted to comment as I continued to provide information. The deceased spoke of a Chinese restaurant as being important to her. Among many other pieces of information, she revealed that her head hurt at the time of her passing. She said volleyball was important to her. These are typical examples of the kind of information that can come through in a reading.

After a few months (the lab was a little slow giving the results), the test was scored by the parents of the deceased and I was able to see the accuracy of my information in the reading. The scoring is important because the sitter scores each piece of information individually. There are a lot of pieces, each scored between a one and a six, one meaning nothing like the deceased, six meaning uniquely specific to the deceased. Then the hundreds of pieces of information are averaged and placed on a scale between one and six to reveal the level of specificity that the medium achieved during the test. It turned out that the deceased was an amazing, beautiful teenage girl who had passed away in a car accident. She had played on her school volleyball team. She had also been in a school production of *The King and I.* Her head hurt from her injuries in the fatal car accident that had occurred after she'd had dinner with her parents at a Chinese restaurant. These were all important details shared by Candace. I won't include all of the details of the reading because there are too many, but you get the gist of what took place that day.

I cannot tell you how much I enjoyed bringing her through and how lucky I felt to be able to experience the love this mother and daughter have for each other. It was an emotional reading, especially because I have daughters and could empathize with the parents of the deceased. People sometimes tell me how they couldn't do what I do; they place a lot of emphasis on the sorrow involved. It is important to me that people understand my view. I believe that I am one of the luckiest people in the world. Even though my job is emotional, I have learned through reading many people how to put aside my own feelings to make room for others to share. When things get really tough, most mediums have found other people, often other mediums, to listen to us as we unload those feelings. I am privileged to be in a position to ease people's pain and reach their loved ones who've passed on. Mediums don't want to be martyrs; we see a lot of good things in our readings. We feel the love between the client and the deceased. We are voyeurs to the special memories held by the deceased. Mothers who pass show pictures like a home movie running in my head. They show their children blowing out candles on birthday cakes. Children who pass let their living parents know how special they felt to have been born to them. Dads show their children small and dancing with them, sometimes standing on their shoes while Dad waltzes with them in his own clumsy way. We see the love, we see the pain, but most important, we see that the dead are not gone.

You will remember that earlier I said there were tests with two different sitters. With the second sitter, I stopped fifteen minutes into the test and told the scientist that I could not complete it because the deceased was someone I recognized from a reading two years before. That was amazing in itself, that I could identify a deceased person from a prior reading. I was given a score of six by the sitter in the first reading, where I connected with Candace, but when the same data was put before the dad from the second reading, who'd lost his son, I received a one, which is great! It means that nothing from the first reading meant anything to the second sitter, even though it meant everything to the first. This showed that specifics that came through could not fit people across the board, as a skeptical mind might argue.

Candace's mom found me, and I am happy that I was able to bring her daughter through to her. Sometimes, though, it is the person from the other side who makes the initial connection, finding me and then guiding their living relative to me as well.

SON

My nineteen-year-old son Brian and his girlfriend traveled more than a thousand miles by car to spend Christmas 2003 with me, his stepdad, and his little sister, then five years old. It was not only a holiday to treasure but one I will surely never forget.

After Christmas was over, my son left Arizona, heading back for New Year's Eve in New Orleans. I didn't hear from my son on New Year's Eve and I sensed that something was terribly wrong, but my son was grown and I didn't want to be an overbearing mom. The next time I heard from Louisiana was four days later, January 4, 2004. It was a detective from Baton Rouge calling me. He told me that my son was dead. In an instant, I was certain my life was over!

After Brian's death, I had three weeks before I had to return to work. Three weeks to wrap my mind and heart around my son's death to try and make sense out of the loss. The loss was so fresh that I was emotionally raw. I was crying incessantly in the car, wherever I drove. There was no end in sight to this unbearable pain and sadness that consumed my heart.

Three weeks into my son's death, my sister-in-law saw Allison's Web site on a local news program and told my husband about it. She suggested that I e-mail Allison. My husband had to do it, as I was not open to anything or anyone because my pain was just so overwhelming. I think it's normal to shut down and put up your guard when you lose someone you love.

On February 7, approximately a month after his death, I received a phone call confirming a date and time to have a reading with Allison. It was scheduled for approximately six weeks after Brian's death. My husband and I left our house early, to find Allison's home and to be there on the dot. Allison greeted my husband and me, stating that our son had been with her for three days. She told us that she had copious notes providing the information communicated to her by Brian that she wanted to confirm with me. I would like to mention that there is no other way and no magic that could produce the knowledge that Allison had about my son. I've always heard that when someone dies, that person is still with you, in your heart. Until I lost my son, I had no real understanding of that idea. In the last five years, I have lost both my parents, an infant child, and my teenage son, and when I say that I did not want to live any longer, I truly mean it. When I tell you that Allison saved my life, again, I mean it.

Allison began describing the coloring, size, and personality characteristics of a dog that she saw standing beside my son. I immediately recognized the dog through the description and fondly reflected on a furry family member that had died before my son. I thought it was pretty funny that right off the bat my son appeared to Allison with one of our four pet schnauzers, named Glitche. I thought it humorous because this was the least favorite of his dogs. I know he knew that it would be important for me to know that Glitche was all right because Glitche meant so much to me. Glitche is now his faithful companion on the other side.

My son said that he wanted me to locate two boxes that would verify much of the reading that I didn't understand at the time. For example, Allison said, "Your son spends a lot of time with Alexander."

I said, "You mean Alexandra."

Allison responded, "No, Alexander."

I wasn't sure about the boxes or Alexander. Two days after the reading, I received a call from an old landlord. We had lived in her building three years before my son's death. She stated that she had found two boxes labeled "keep-sakes" along with the name "Brian." She wanted to know if I knew who that was. I guess since it had been so long, she didn't remember my son's name. Her call was a godsend. As the shock of the call settled in, I pondered what could be in the boxes.

Anyone who's lost anyone knows how valuable get-ting that call was to me. To be able to have something that belonged to my son and to know that he orchestrated that gift from the other side to let me know he is still here with me was invaluable. Not just anything, but childhood mementos—it doesn't get any better than that.

I immediately retrieved the boxes. Upon opening the first, I found a folder with a project that Brian had completed in school, titled "Old Families of Louisiana." The biography of "Alexander Stirling from the 1700's" was the first thing that I laid my eyes on. He was a family ancestor whom my son had wanted to know more about.

Allison also described seeing a large body of water with paddlewheel boats. "This is where your son likes to be. He spends time there."

Allison said that she's never been to Louisiana or the Mississippi River. She described every detail of the area to a tee. Keep in mind that she knew nothing of our Louisiana background and I have no accent.

Allison went on to explain how my son had died, that he had been administered something that he had had a bad reaction to. She described how quickly it happened and how he left this world in no pain.

She described his spirit, his personality; she used words and expressions that he would use.

Allison gave me names of songs that Brian would play for me, and after his passing he did play them consistently for months. Whether I was in the car or an elevator, I heard the songs that she named. She explained how spirits have almost an electric energy and that they can manipulate other objects with electric energy like computers, radios, and such to give signs that they're still around.

She described my son's relationship with his little sister, before he died and after.

She talked about an older man whom he plays checkers with. When I spoke with my son's biological dad in

Louisiana, I was informed that his great-grandfather played checkers all the time.

Allison also said, "He says he still calls you on your phone."

I immediately grabbed my purse and pulled out my cell phone. I had to show her the text message that Brian had sent me *after* his passing. The message said that he loved me. Allison had confirmed that he had indeed called me when he left the text message on my cell phone. This occurred three days after he had died. The message was not traceable. In October, nine months after his death, he text-messaged me again when my dad died. I believe he was letting me know that he was around my dad. The calls would pop my son's name up on the screen.

Allison continued, "Your son says he misses barbecued ribs."

She explained that those who have passed often come through with their favorite food dishes. Kind of like a calling card and also because favorite foods bring good feelings in life.

This is his favorite food in the whole world. When we have ribs for dinner, Brian always gives us a sign that he's with us. Whether it's lights flickering or a small animal running up to us in our yard and looking eye to eye with us.

Allison confirmed that my daughter's little toy airplane with no batteries would light up and turn around on top of our television. This was a regular occurrence. Allison validated what we had suspected, that my son was the culprit.

Apparently, by affecting objects, spirits communicate that they're around the objects' owners. The toy is my daughter's, so my son is just letting us know he's watching over her.

Allison gave me many other messages and family members' names that I validated for her. There are too many to mention, but the signs that are there—daily, weekly, all the time—are what mean the most to me. That's the gift that Allison gave to me. She put me on the same page energetically as Brian so that I can appreciate the signs instead of dismissing them. Allison's recognition of signs that I already suspected were from Brian, without her having heard them from me, confirmed to me that my son is contacting me. The truth is, in my heart I already knew this. I *know* that my son is around me always. Now I can enjoy the signs and talk to my son knowing that he hears me.

Not only did Brian contact Allison, he communicated through her. My son's reaching out to me saved my life. Was I skeptical? Of course. Did I want it to be true? Again, of course. However, I had no idea the amount of detailed information that would be passed from my son to Allison. I found myself amazed at the absolute proof that my son still existed. That proof would surface over and over again, reassuring me that my son would never leave his mom. He's not gone.

If by telling my story and sharing my relationship with Allison, I can help one person who has lost a child to cope a little better, then Brian would be happy. I truly feel that what happens in life is all a part of a bigger plan, bigger than any of us can comprehend. I am Catholic. I always believed in heaven and hell. I don't have all the answers about religion or spirits, but I am telling you that I don't think I could have moved forward without Allison DuBois's giving me a little nudge in the right direction. She helped me to understand that my child is still with me, watching over his sister, giving us signs all the time that he's around. Does it still hurt? Of course. Do you still miss your child? Yes! You always will; your children are a part of you. I still cry and sometimes get so sad that I literally cry myself to sleep. You always look back and wonder what you could've or should've done differently. Would it have changed this tragic event? Did you do something wrong in life? But my son told Allison to tell me something very important. His words were "Mom, you couldn't have prevented my passing. It was out of your hands." He also said that he knows I love him and that I'm a good mom. So when I go to bed at night, I can lay my head on that for comfort.

Allison has a gift. It is a gift from God. It's been a year and a half since Brian's death. I now spend much of my time telling stories about him, laughing about him, remembering him in the most wonderful ways. I know that I couldn't have changed the fact that he was slated to leave this world when he did and that gives me some peace. I have emerged in a positive way since my readings with Allison. If I can touch one reader and help that person, then my pain becomes more bearable because my son's tragic death wasn't in vain.

Once you believe that your child's spirit is truly with you, you will be more open to signs. The signs are there, but you have to believe in their existence. I'm a fortunate woman to have had an incredible son for nineteen years, and I'm blessed to have a seven-year-old daughter. I know how lucky I am to have them. Still, in the first reading that I had, my son stated that he knew that I wanted to be with him and that I was thinking that I didn't want to live any longer, but that he would give me signs all the time and help me to move forward. He would give me his strength so that I could make it through the day. He reminded me that I need to be here for his sister. He said when it's my time, when I'm *reeeaaallly* old, that he'd be there to welcome me into heaven. So I'll keep making the barbecued ribs and talking to my daughter about Brian. He is a part of me that I will never let go.

A Persistent Young Man

I will always remember the persistent young man who inhabited my house for three days. If I went in my backyard, he was there. Walked in the kitchen, he was there. He would pop in and out of my house and yard throughout the day, demanding my attention, standing before me waiting for me to drop everything for him, making me feel an urgency within to act as a secretary and take notes for him. By the time his mom and stepdad arrived for their reading, I was relieved to relay his messages so that I could have some alone time again. Just kidding! He was only in my house because he knew that his parents would be there soon. I don't usually summon the dead. They most often use me as a go-between, knowing that their loved ones are making their way toward me. I believe my clients have been brought to me by the deceased through strange "coincidences." Sometimes the dead whisper in the ear of the living, saying, "Her, go to her."

It was interesting how Brian's mom even got an appointment with me. I was booked for almost a year at that time. Somehow my booker, who was learning how to use her computer, had slid the grieving mother into a cancellation spot. She was on the waiting list, but not near the top, oops! Not only that, but I have a policy that three months need to pass after a death before I do the reading so that there's time for things to unfold in the client's life and to give the client some time to find their footing again after the loss. It had only been a few weeks for her, which I found out during the reading. Brian did pretty good orchestrating that one!

Brian, who knew how much his mom needed to hear from him, pulled a lot of strings, which just shows the lengths he'll go to for his mom.

What I remember the most about the reading is the moment when I told her, "He still reaches you on your phone."

She seemed a little shocked. Then she reached into her

purse and pulled out her cell phone. She ran through her saved messages, and there was a text message sent from Brian *after* his death. His name was on the screen with the message, "I love you mom."

I was also struck by the boy's mention of the boxes that would confirm the information that I gave the mother. It's always hard to look at a client and say, "It'll make sense to you at some point." This is an important part of the process of a reading, because being told something that has yet to happen reinforces that the spirit was there.

I never question spirits in these circumstances because I've seen them work their magic before. I look at my clients and reassure them as I say, "Really, they'll come through for you."

I also remember feeling my client's pain and also feeling Brian's attempt to ease it for her. Looking at my client, I saw the same face that I see every time that I read a person who's lost a child. I'm glad I not only got to know my client but also had the pleasure of knowing her mischievous son. I'm also not advising everyone to run out and book with a medium. I'm just trying to give others a glimpse into a place they themselves may not be able to see. And I want to reassure those who mourn lost children that their children are always a part of them, even after death. For those of you who know that your children are still with you after death, talk to them. They can hear you. If you decide to book a medium, do your homework. I find word of mouth from a family member or trusted friend to be the best indicator of a medium's ability.

I often see parents who carry a heavy burden. It's the burden of "What if? What if I had known? What if I could have changed things?" I'm talking about parents of children who have some specific self-destructive behavior that leads to their death. This was the case with Christine.

This wonderful woman lost her precious teenage daughter to addiction. Let me state that addiction was only a part of this girl. She was also tenacious, intelligent, beautiful, and sensitive.

Christine's daughter Dallas had a chemical imbalance. Because of Dallas's age, it's easy to see why Christine thought that Dallas was just experiencing "growing pains." Most parents can relate to this, as they are often told by their friends, "Oh, she'll grow out of it." Unfortunately, some kids are not given the chance to. Dallas, like many kids, had experimented with drugs. As far as Christine knew, Dallas had only tried smoking marijuana. But Dallas's drug use had turned into something much bigger. It had evolved into an addiction to crystal meth. By the time Christine found out about the severity of her daughter's problem, it was too late. I explained to Christine that many people will benefit from her story, recognizing similarities between her story and their own. It's important for people to grasp that many people with chemical imbalances turn to drugs or alcohol to "find balance." From my experience bringing through the deceased who had chemical imbalances, I have noticed that the more severe the imbalance, the more they reached for drug or drink.

There is a vital purpose to Christine's story—to prevent any preventable deaths and to teach by example. I want you all to know that there is a ripple effect to every death, one that touches many and helps some that are in jeopardy to be pushed back to shore.

CHRISTINE

I never thought that Dallas wouldn't outlive me. She was definitely choosing the difficult path, but we were always hopeful that she would "grow up" and become the beautiful, fun daughter that we had before. We didn't know that she had been using crystal meth for more than six months before it took her away from us. This is how devastating and quick this drug can be. It can change and take a life without remorse or warning. If any parents think that their child is involved with drugs, I beg them to do *whatever* it takes to save their child. I know that I wish every day that I had done more or somehow could have saved my daughter.

My husband and I have two other children, Tori and Mason, and *they* are why we keep going. I thank God for them every day.

I used to pray to God every night for my children to be safe, happy, and healthy. After Dallas died, I was telling a friend of mine at work about my prayers and how God hadn't listened to me. She responded with "Have you ever thought that maybe Dallas is happy now?"

Those few words have stayed with me. I think they are true. Dallas wasn't happy here when she was alive. The next best thing to having Dallas with us is having Allison talk to her and relay to us her messages letting us know that she is in a much better place. I know now that she is much more content where she is.

There were some specific pieces of information that Allison gave me in my reading that really touched me. When I feel sad, I can look back on them to remind myself that my little girl is still with me.

One of the first things out of Allison's mouth was "Dallas is around a male who skateboards, a younger male whom she loves."

Her brother Mason, who is only eleven, skateboards just about every day of his life! It meant a lot for Dallas to acknowledge her brother.

Allison mentioned an "Ashley" connected to Dallas. She said that Dallas is around Ashley now. Ashley is her closest girl cousin, my brother's daughter. Again, it's comforting to know that she's still with us.

Allison also mentioned a "Jason" and that he may be someone whom I "blame." This is the name of the boy she was living with at the time of her death, a boy who I believe was giving her the drugs. He died one year after Dallas as a result of his own poor choices.

Allison stated, "Dallas likes to spend time around your dad, Christine."

Well, my dad lives in Arkansas and we had just spent a long weekend with him. I guess she was there with us!

Allison also said, "She is around a favorite uncle."

My brother died 360 days before her. They were like brother and sister, so there is no doubt in my mind that they are together having a grand ole time. I sat with Allison as she provided me with information that validated to me that my daughter is doing well and is still an "active" member of our family.

Allison also brought through my brother Eric, who had passed away. It was the first time that Allison and I had met, and *wow,* did he ever come through loud and clear. The very first thing she said was "Now don't take this the wrong way. He is laughing and saying he is a menace to society."

That is so Eric! After he died, I could hear him laughing like he was standing right next to me for at least two weeks. Allison also mentioned a Ron "connected" to Eric. Ron is our dad's name and also the name of one of Eric's close friends. I could feel Eric there in the room with us. He had a huge presence in life, as he still does in the afterlife!

Thank you, Allison, for reconnecting my family.

Dallas

In February of 2003 I was asked to do a reading at a news station that would be taped to air. The news station would pick the sitter, who would sit behind me during a controlled experiment. I was up for the challenge, so I accepted. Aside from any science that I participated in, it was always the sitter and the soothed soul that were the greatest incentive for me to participate.

When I arrived at the news station, I met a producer named Jim, who seemed friendly but guarded. He pulled up a chair for me, and I perched myself on it. I was a little nervous. To calm my nerves, I pulled out one of my favorite gifts of all time, my iPod. I put in my tiny earphones and tried to go to a more relaxed place in my head, tuning out the hustle and bustle of the cameramen, spectators, and others. If a medium is too distracted by surroundings, we tend to lose some of the information that we receive in readings. I had my big, white pad of paper to jot down the information that I receive before a reading about the sitter and the people they have asked to hear from. I was given the signal that my sitter was in place behind me ready to go. As I moved through the information piece by piece, I was so focused on receiving, I was unaware that my sitter behind me was in tears. When we were finished, I stood up and turned around to hug my sitter, who turned out to be a woman named Christine. She reminded me very much of my own friends, and I liked her immediately. I also liked her daughter Dallas, whom I had brought through. I had also brought through her brother who had recently passed. He was a kick in the pants. Her daughter was sorry she had left so soon but was more concerned about her mom. I would not see Christine again for almost two years.

After the news segment aired, I was asked by the news

producer if I would read his wife, Wendy, as a Valentine's Day gift from him. I obliged. His wife was a young woman with long brown hair and eyes that were big, friendly, green welcome mats. She was tall and thin, with an air of laughter wrapped around her. She sat down and I read her for an hour. Afterward, I walked her out. Little did I know that she would become one of my closest friends. She was the person who had suggested to her TV producer husband that he invite Christine to be the sitter. So, almost two years later, while I was working on this chapter, Wendy said, "Why don't you call Christine and share her story?"

"Oh, I don't want to bother her."

"Allison, it's no bother. She'd probably like to talk about Dallas."

This led to Christine's coming back to see me. I told her that I was thinking of a follow-up reading for her. Christine replied that she had received the information she needed from Dallas the first time we met and that I shouldn't go to any trouble. I said, "Well that's nice to hear, but Dallas showed up to talk to me last night and I have five pages of notes from her, if you want them."

So I went through the pages with Christine, and it was great to see that her daughter was in an even better place than before. Dallas was also still giving messages to reassure her mom and remind her that she remains around her family out of love, not because she's bound here for some sad reason. Christine's brother who passed is a real joker and caught my attention with his Cheshire cat grin. Her brother showed me himself riding around a lake on a Jet Ski, waving, smiling, and, as he put it, "living." Dallas said she was with Christine's wonderful granddad and that "he died far too soon." Only one of Christine's granddads had passed. He had died of a heart attack beside her crib when he was in his forties. So it was very nice for Christine to know that her daughter was with her granddad. Dallas kept talking about the VW bug and said she would have had one had she lived longer. Christine found this touching since she herself had had one when she was younger and she used to tell her kids about it and all of her adventures in it. This led to Christine's affection for "slug bug," which is a game that she played regularly with her kids. It seemed that Dallas was also saying that she really wanted to be like her mom, which is the biggest compliment that any parent can receive. It's the obscure little details that can carry the biggest impact in a reading. The details that would mean nothing to another person mean everything to the bereaved. I am quite sure I will be hearing from Dallas again, and I look forward to that day.

All in the Family

This story is unusual for many reasons. It deals with the death of a beloved son born into a family of mediums/psychics who span at least three generations and without a doubt many more. It's important for people to understand what it's like to "know" that something bad is going to happen and not be able to stop it. I think many people will be able to relate to this feeling because most parents are innately connected to their children on many levels. From the moment their child is born and, for some people, before that, there is an unbreakable bond. People who would say they've never predicted anything in their life seem to sense when their children are in trouble. So, whether you're a medium/psychic or just highly connected to those you love, it's not hard to relate to Mark Ireland's loss of his son. We may also empathize with his ability to embrace his son's soul after his death and admire his ability to begin to turn his family's pain into healing for others. I also think that it's nice to see a dad's perspective. Mark has been gracious enough to share his with us.

FATHERS AND SONS

It occurred to me that my background is probably very different from that of most other people who experience a reading with Allison. You see, my father was a prominent psychic-medium, so I experienced the phenomenon of predictions coming to pass on a firsthand basis every day growing up. From the 1950s until his passing in 1992, Dad counseled celebrities like Mae West and Amanda Blake, in addition to high-ranking government officials, who had total trust in his guidance. My father appeared on television programs, gave lectures, and demonstrated his abilities worldwide. He was also a deeply spiritual minister who worked with religious leaders from all faiths, using his gifts to spread the message, "There is no death and there are no dead." Despite my dad's outstanding abilities and achievements, very few people today know the name Richard Ireland. Looking back, I guess Dad was ahead of his time, a sort of trailblazer, if you will.

Living with someone who has these gifts is a double-edged sword. When your father knows *everything* that's going on, you really can't get away with much. On the other hand, seeing my dad's gifts displayed on a daily basis, I came to fully appreciate that psychic phenomena and spirit communication are real. It was comforting to know that there's something more than just this brief physical existence.

Moving into adulthood, I suppressed any personal psychic leanings and focused on a mainstream lifestyle. While I experienced intuitive feelings on many occasions, it was rare for me to trust them. So while I loved my father, I deliberately chose a different and more stable path than a life centered on the metaphysical. I was practical, driven, and focused on business and family, pushing aside part of my lineage to concentrate on my own life. Working hard over the years, I enjoyed success, which allowed me to build a beautiful home for my family—a loving wife and two wonderful sons, one in high school and the other in college. In January 2004, however, my calculated, comfortable life was rocked to its foundation.

My younger son, Brandon, had just turned eighteen and was entering the final semester of his senior year in high school. Good-natured and easy to please, Brandon was invariably considerate of others. He was tall and lanky, with long, curly brown hair and eyes reflecting a loving and caring nature. His strong jaw line, dimpled chin, and the ridge on his forehead were a fresh minting of my features.

Brandon had become quite proficient on the bass guitar after six years of lessons. He showed a strong aptitude for mathematics, which correlated to his exceptional musical skills. His mathematical ability also led him to an interest in physics, which he intended to study in college. Brandon's college plans were well outlined and bolstered by good SAT scores. In concert with his friends, he was excited and ready to embark on future goals.

Despite my pragmatic nature, I was disturbed by vivid premonitions that came as a feeling of certainty, a gut feeling of impending disaster, on the morning of January 10, 2004. Brandon shared his intention to embark on a very difficult hike with friends to the summit of the McDowell Mountains near our home in Scottsdale, Arizona. He enjoyed hiking as a regular hobby and had hiked three times earlier that week.

Because of my strong feelings, I asked Brandon to stay home.

In response, my son looked me and said, "We're going, Dad," as if to convey the message "Stop worrying."

I got the sense that my son thought I was just being a worried dad.

So, in spite of my warnings, Brandon began his trek toward the McDowell Mountains with four of his good friends. On that particular day, ominously strong winds pushed pollutants from the Greater Phoenix valley toward the mountains where Brandon was hiking. The impure air made the vigorous climb all the more stressful. Brandon suffered a severe asthma attack, which resulted in reduced levels of oxygen in his bloodstream. I was later told that Brandon had rested in an effort to regain his strength and ability to breathe. Brandon also used his prescription inhaler, hoping to improve his deteriorating respiration. Unfortunately, these actions were ineffective, and Brandon's condition grew progressively worse.

Evidently, Brandon attempted to climb back down to the base of the mountain with two of his friends (the other two had gone ahead at a faster pace), which further depleted the oxygen supply he needed to sustain his heart and brain. He became light-headed and had to rest repeatedly. The gradual decline in blood oxygen levels eventually caused Brandon's heart to fail. Because of the unique symptoms, which included a rapid heartbeat and numbness of limbs, neither Brandon nor his good friend Stuart recognized his condition as an asthma attack. While Brandon used his inhaler to see if it might help, both boys thought something else was wrong because the symptoms were unlike anything my son had ever experienced. I later learned that Brandon was joking the entire time and never seemed panicked. Apparently, he failed to recognize the severity of the situation, which turned out to be a blessing in disguise. Just before collapsing, Brandon told Stuart that "Everything was shining."

This statement evokes images of what heaven might have looked like to my son.

Needless to say, I repeatedly kicked myself for failing to heed my intuitive warning. Although I initially thought I might have been able to alter the outcome, I now believe that the outcome was a matter of destiny. Perhaps the warning was intended to prepare me emotionally for the inevitable. The fact is that I could have demanded that Brandon stay home on Saturday only to have him hike on Sunday with the same conclusion. In fact, I've come to recognize that there is no value in playing the blame game.

I love my son Brandon more than words can describe, and I've had great difficulty imagining life without him. After his passing, I would often break down and cry and still do on occasion. Nothing can prepare a parent for the loss of a child.

After losing Brandon, I recalled teachings that my dad shared many years ago, teachings focused on God's love and the continuity of life. My father wrote books and even documented his own psychic work, leaving behind a legacy of valued training materials. I found renewed interest in these writings and began poring over them.

I also recalled that spirit communication was available

to me. Immediately I called my uncle Robert, a medium psychic and retired minister. I asked my uncle, "Please share anything you may receive or feel that pertains to Brandon. Any information that you receive on him at all."

At about 2 p.m., on Monday, January 12, 2004, I was standing in the Desert Hills mortuary in Scottsdale, Arizona, when my cell phone rang. Realizing that the call was from my uncle, I felt a mixed sense of hope and anxiety. I then listened with great anticipation as my uncle proceeded to tell me, "I tried hard to make a connection last night but got nothing. This morning, however, your dad came to me during meditation. He told me that Brandon's heart failed due to a lack of oxygen and, while he experienced shortness of breath, Brandon suffered no pain. When he first left his body, Brandon was confused, but your dad came to meet him and helped him adjust. [Sometimes when a person dies, it takes him or her a while to realize what happened.] Brandon also had a message for you and Susie. He wants you to know that you were the best parents he ever could have had."

This might seem like a general statement to most, but coupled with the specific details that my uncle had already given pertaining to Brandon and my personal relationship with my uncle, I had no reason to doubt him. As a matter of fact, coming from him, the information meant even more, and it was something that I needed to hear. While we were still reeling from the loss of Brandon, my uncle's words provided immeasurable comfort for my family.

When I spoke to my uncle, there had been nothing confirmed by the authorities about the cause of Brandon's
death. The authorities would not share any information with
us regarding the suspected cause, nor were they even willing to speculate. It was about a week after speaking to my
uncle that I received validation of my uncle's description of
Brandon's cause of death. When I spoke to the physician
who performed the autopsy, she explained that Brandon's
death was attributed to a severe asthma attack. In an effort
to process more oxygen, his lungs had become oversized to
the point of nearly touching in the middle. Evidently, this
condition occurs only in cases of drowning and severe
asthma. Brandon's inability to process oxygen eventually
led to cardiac arrest, thus the official cause of death
matched the description given by my uncle. Not knowing
our son's cause of death for a week was terrible; my uncle's
assurance that it was a natural death was comforting at a
time when nobody else could give us the answer to the
question, "Why did our son die?"

At this time, I also felt inspired to begin daily meditation
in hopes of enhancing my perceptive abilities and connecting with Brandon. I didn't expect to develop skills anywhere
near my dad's level but did aspire to become more "connected." As a result of these efforts, my sensitivity became
heightened to some degree.

Just a few days after Brandon's passing, I sat meditating quietly. During this time I saw an image of Brandon's
face, which seemed to be surrounded by warmth and joy. I

can only describe this feeling as a simultaneous melding of different sensory input. After the vision of Brandon's face I *saw* a symbol, which was a cross with an oval loop at the top. I was not familiar with this particular image, so I searched for information on the Internet. As a result of my research, I learned that the cross was an ankh, an ancient Egyptian symbol that predates the cross of the crucifixion. The lower cross portion of the symbol represents physical life, while the oval loop portion at the top symbolizes eternal life. Ultimately, I believe that the message was a symbolic way of confirming that Brandon is indeed alive and well.

My older son, Steven, also began meditating after Brandon died. About a week into the process—two weeks after his brother's passing—Steven experienced a vivid dream that I believe was an astral experience. Astrals, commonly referred to as "out-of-body experiences," are very different from everyday dreams. They are astonishingly lucid experiences. During astrals, our senses are exceedingly sharp and surroundings seem exceptionally real. While in this state, our physical body remains asleep while our soul or "spiritual body" (described by the apostle Paul, in the New Testament) travels in other realms, dimensions, or "planes."

While asleep, Steven heard music emanating from our living room. Walking toward that room, he saw Brandon playing the bass guitar, a previously common scene in our home. Steven immediately ran to his brother and gave him a hug, noting that the embrace was so real, he actually *felt* the fabric of Brandon's shirt. Steven then asked Brandon, "What's it like?" and Brandon replied, "At first it was so weird, but now it feels incredible." Brandon then said to Steven, "Why don't you come visit me more often?"

After the encounter with his brother, while still physically asleep, Steven experienced hovering above his own body and observing the time on a clock in his room. As he awoke, Steven opened his eyes and looked at the clock, finding that the time was exactly the same as what he had just seen in his "dream" without the aid of his physical senses. It seemed that the validation with the clock allowed Steven to recognize that what he had experienced with his brother was very real.

My wife also experienced a profound connection. While sitting alone at the foot of our bed, Susie suddenly felt Brandon's presence very strongly. She was then able to see Brandon, as a shadow figure, discernible through her peripheral vision for about thirty seconds. She was absolutely certain that this was Brandon: she could *feel* it. One day later, Susie received a phone call from a musician friend, James Linton, who was shaken and needed to talk. Before even hearing of Susie's experiences, James described a similar set of circumstances, where he felt the presence of someone else while recording music in his studio. James also saw a shadow figure through his peripheral vision in the exact same manner as Susie had.

In February 2004 I was contacted by one of my dad's friends, who called to share his condolences and provide a helpful suggestion. This gentleman, Jerry Conser, asked me how I was doing and then said, "Mark, I know of a quality medium in Phoenix who can help you get in touch with your son." Intrigued by Jerry's words, I listened with a sense of heightened anticipation as he continued, "Her name is Allison DuBois." I was stunned by Jerry's comments because I'd just seen a news clip about Allison one day earlier.

As a result of Jerry's call, I contacted Allison's assistant to arrange a reading. It was a few months before I could see her, because she was booked through the balance of the year, but the experience was well worth the wait. Allison provided highly compelling evidence that my father and son were both still quite alive, as evidenced in the following reading excerpts:

Brandon's presence was immediately apparent in Allison's first words, "I see a son connected to you. I'm not sure if he passed or if I'm seeing a son who is yet to be born." Given that Allison was unaware that I had a son on the other side, I was greatly encouraged by this start and hoping for even more.

Allison continued, "Your dad is referencing a Susan as being connected to you. He notes that he is around Susan. Do you understand?" Greatly impressed, I responded, "Why yes, that's my wife!"

Allison then delivered one of the most compelling validations of the day, speaking to a matter that was a complete secret, "I see him signing a book and handing it over to you. I believe this was his book and he is handing it over to you.

Do you understand this?" Delighted beyond words, I burst out, "Totally!"

Just a week earlier, I'd been contacted by one of my father's friends, who handed me an unpublished manuscript that my father authored back in 1973. Before receiving this call, I was completely unaware that the book, entitled *ESP Development Course,* even existed. Apparently, just before his passing, my dad asked this friend to hold the book for safekeeping. Now for some inexplicable reason, *twelve years later,* this person suddenly felt compelled to share the book with me. I started thinking this was just too coincidental to be a coincidence.

Allison assumed a new path, which garnered my immediate attention: "Your dad mentions 'having the boy.' Your son is with your dad, and he says 'that's how it should be.' " This statement made me flash back to my uncle's description of how my dad greeted Brandon at the time of his passing. The validation was even more significant because I knew that Allison was unaware that I'd lost a son. (Before the reading, I had verified that Jerry Conser had not spoken to her.)

Now sharing information from my son, Allison said, "Twenty-five years is being shown as important for you and your wife. Have you hit your twenty-fifth anniversary?" Pleasantly surprised, I responded, "Yes, we had our twenty-fifth anniversary, on June thirtieth." Allison then said, "Happy anniversary. These are the things that matter to them after they pass—the happy times." I was thrilled by this wonderful validation, which referenced a milestone event that had occurred less than two months earlier.

I then began a determined pursuit of top mediums throughout America and Europe in a personal search for answers to some very deep questions. In the course of my readings with all the mediums, I was amazed at the specific, accurate information that was provided. Even more compelling was the consistency of the messages that began to overlay and form a sort of mosaic.

I also found it therapeutic to talk about Brandon with other people and to allow myself to cry whenever the feeling came. My wife, son, and I like to be around other people who knew and loved Brandon and are not afraid to talk about him, sharing special memories. You may find that some people are afraid to discuss topics pertaining to loved ones who have passed. What these folks don't understand is that we want to talk about our mothers, fathers, sons, and daughters who have crossed over because it helps us feel connected to them and it keeps them fresh in our minds. If you encounter people who shy away from mentioning those who have passed, give them permission to talk openly by letting them know that you want to share stories about your loved ones. Ultimately, there is no "one size fits all" approach to the healing process, but I hope my story will help others who are struggling through loss.

Connecting with Brandon

I remember the day that I met Mark. He was a good-looking man whose hair had just begun to pepper in a very distinguished way. He was a little anxious and very focused. I invited him to have a seat in my office, and I explained to him that if he sees me scribbling on a pad of paper, it's my protocol when I read. Writing down the information helps me to focus and "process out" the energy that I'm bringing through, which is the deceased. He seemed very pleasant. He reminded me a little bit of the engineers that my husband worked with, so I knew he was very intelligent and a little aloof.

I began his reading by getting a "son" connection to him. I asked him if he had a son who had died. I couldn't tell if his son had died or if this was a son yet to be. He said yes, his son had passed away. I remember feeling drowning, heaviness in the lungs. I felt an urgency around the son. The problem for me was that Mark had another son who's living, so I wanted to be thorough. I said, "If your deceased son didn't have asthma or pass with a feeling of water in the lungs, then keep an eye on your living son." Mark then said that his son who had passed had asthma and the M.E. indeed had said that it would have felt as though there were water in his lungs even though he died in the desert. I also remember very well that Mark's dad made an appearance, saying that he's with his grandson as he should be. I was very happy when Mark's deceased dad mentioned the name "Susan" and said he is fond of her and is connected to her. Mark said this is his wife's name and was happy to hear his dad acknowledge her. I was very moved by Mark's love for his son. He is without question a wonderful dad. I have no doubt that Mark's son and dad will be there for Mark when his time comes for a reunion. I've since met Susan and Mark's son Steven. They are a uniquely centered family, not only spiritually healthy but a lot of fun to be around. I won't forget that reading because I brought through my first professional psychic-medium. He was very easy to understand and to relay messages from. Interestingly, skeptics are like pulling mud through a colander. I think the more open-minded and spiritual people must be doing something right, because they certainly are more pleasant in death.

When I asked Mark to contribute his story to this chapter, I asked him to include advice for people walking his same path. (I asked the same from all of the parents in this chapter; their responses are immeasurably helpful.) Mark not only "gets it," his account is eloquent and heartfelt: "Those you've lost are not gone, and you will never be alone."

Lost Children

While writing this chapter, I tried to be thorough and cover different parents and their own experiences, as well as mine. I also know that some children who die pass at the hands of others. This is a different kind of pain, often because the parents have a face that represents the person who took their child's life. Sometimes parents don't have that, and they spend a lot of time sizing people up, wondering if they're looking at the face of the person who unjustly took their child's life.

In 2005 I was faced with one of the most rewarding yet heavy experiences that I have ever faced. I was asked to be a guest speaker at a grief support group. I never hesitated to accept their invitation, and I was honored to be asked. I was also well aware that this task would not be easy and would be a challenge to recover from. When the night came for me to speak at the meeting, I knew that I would meet many wonderful people, both the living and those who had passed.

Joe and I pulled into the parking lot behind the building where the group meeting was being held. I found it hard to collect myself to face the overwhelming nature of the roomful of traumatic deaths that awaited me. Previously I had "read" for people who had lost their children to murder, but this was on a much larger scale with a clear focus on murder. I didn't want to walk in looking shaken. I was there to comfort the parents. I reminded myself that any empathy that I felt for them didn't even come close to what they had been through. So I took a deep breath and walked through the door.

I asked myself, If I lost a child in this way, what are the words that could bring some relief?

My goal in coming to the meeting was to send the people there home in a better place energetically than when they first walked through the door.

I stood in a room that had many broken hearts inside. I could feel and see the kids who had had their lives cut short. We were seated in a large circle, and behind the parents and siblings of the murder victims stood the figures of the deceased. Some had their hand on their dad's shoulder; some were just smiling at those who came for them. They were all there, ready to come through and have their words be heard by their parents. There were children who had been adults at the time of their death; nevertheless they were somebody's child. There were boys and girls of all ages, and they knew that I could see them. I suspect they are there every week to support their parents. They were children of all skin colors and heights, children who'd died of gunshots wounds, died in hand-to-hand combat after being attacked, died in many terrible ways at the hands of others.

I was given a little white stuffed bear with angel wings that was made specifically for this support group. I clung to this little bear for comfort and to keep my focus. I searched the faces of the people present, hoping I could somehow relieve a small part of their pain. In this room full of people who'd lost a child in the most painful way, I thought, This is why I do what I do!

I asked those who had died to please come through "loud and clear" because I would only have a couple of minutes for each living person. I have to tell the dead exactly what I need from them so they can work with me. I started off by sharing that sometimes siblings like to come through to their brothers and sisters through music that they play on the radio, or they tell me that in death they passed their record collection to their sibling. This is one way to let the living know they are still with them. Often "their song" will play in the most obscure place; other times it will play everywhere you go. I shared with the group that people who liked to talk on the phone in life tend to be behind the phone calls where we find silence on the other end when we pick up. This is the deceased's way of telling us that they can still reach us. Many present acknowledged having experiences where they "knew" it was their child saying, "I'm still here."

I spent part of the evening trying to explain to parents why someone would shoot and kill their child. I had to answer the question "Why would God let a child die?" One boy who died was killed by his own parent. "Why?" is an enormous question. From what I can tell, it's because without loss we don't appreciate what we have. Premature death causes a tidal wave of emotions that inspire others to hold their children more, some to start support groups to help others like them, others to fight for tougher laws that will in turn prevent the deaths of many others. There is always a backlash from pain that creates a stronger consciousness.

We are human and are feeling beings who sometimes get caught up in ourselves and we forget why we are here to begin with. We are here to make it better for someone else, to learn what matters in life, to see and experience love. With love comes loss, but that loss is temporary and the love stays forever. Sometimes this is little comfort for the grieving, but it is something to think about. Grief brings people together in search of happiness again. Grief builds our awareness, and relationships change.

After an emotional evening with this group, I felt both wiped out and renewed. I left the meeting having gotten to know a group of wonderful people, both the living and the deceased. I looked deep into the eyes of people who are forced to be resilient without any choice in the matter. I studied their faces, which I will always remember, and I willingly felt their pain. I wasn't going to be one of those who distance themselves from these people. I would be one who embraces them, even if it meant sharing their pain. Sometimes you have to feel someone's pain in order to help take some of it away. The members hugged me good-bye and walked out the door with smiles on their faces. I didn't solve all of their problems, but I did help cast light on the faces of their children so they could be seen on that special night.

At that meeting I was asked, as I often am, about "dreams" where the people we love appear. I explained that a dream is like being able to fly or drive a race car through the sky. When someone who died appears in our dreams, it's a visit. It's that person's way of telling us that he or she is still with us and a part of our life. People I've talked to who've had this experience know the feeling and how unmistakable a dream visit is. You can feel the difference in your heart because your heart feels lighter. Those who have died just want us to acknowledge that we know that they're still here. If you feel tension or irritation from the spirit, it's for that reason. Once they're acknowledged, they relax, and you won't get such a feeling of urgency.

Also, please remember that when you lose people you love, they still continue to share in your day. They will still sit in their favorite chair. They'll still talk to you. Their personality will largely determine what signs they choose to send you. Do you want to share sorrow and pain with them daily? I think they would like to share in your good times. Of course, you're going to have bad days from time to time, but if you make an effort to share a good day with those who've passed, they get to take part in your joy. Nothing makes them happier. Talk to those who have passed and laugh with them again. Pore over their pictures, and you'll find that one will stand out. That's how they communicate to you what they look like now. Love those you love enough to live for them.

Your loved ones don't want you to suffer for the rest of your life, paying homage to them through your tears. They sit there with you while you cry, and the harder you cry, the louder you get. But if you are drowning them out with sobs, then how can they be heard? Allow peace to enter your heart, take a deep breath, and ask them to let you know they're with you. They will find a way. They want to continue to share in your life and in the memories you're making.

Live life "large" for yourself. That allows them to continue living.

As many of you know, my dad passed away in 2002. Sometimes, to feel closer to him, I eat a big cheeseburger or go to the movies. Why? Because burgers and movies are two things we used to enjoy together when I was little. The more connections you make to those who've passed, the stronger you'll feel their presence. By extending your energy to them and embracing their presence in your life, you will find some of the pain you carry slip away, to be replaced by the love your loved ones still have for you.

Visits are a fantastic gift from the person who passed. When a child dies, the loved ones experience grief in many different ways. Usually mothers feel torn to pieces from within and, bound by grief, can't move forward. They have a lump in their throat that appeared the day they lost their child and it has never left them. They often can't speak without crying. They remember holding their baby in their arms and making a favorite sandwich when the child was small. (Children usually keep those favorites no matter how old they get, because their mom made it for them and that made them feel loved.)

People mourning the loss of a loved one feel guilt for having a good day, which turns into a no-win situation. It is important, healthy, and necessary to relearn how to live after any great loss. Parents who've lost children must move forward for the rest of their family. It is easy for the siblings and other family members of the deceased to see only the focus on the child who died; the living may feel unseen and unheard. Those who've passed on don't want their death to take the focus off the living. Parents need to own that their child wants Mom and Dad to be happy and wants to share their good days with them but will also share their bad days, if that's all there is. Mothers gave life to their child and are challenged to allow themselves to move forward and know that their child is indeed still with them. Easier said than done: this is by no means an easy task. But it's important for anyone mourning a loss to make an effort to move through the pain for their own well-being. Moms, or anybody who has lost someone they love, have to find a new way of loving that person, since hugs and kisses are no longer an option. Talk to those who've passed, eat their favorite food, or find a picture that draws you in and helps you to share their love. Remember, they can hear you and touch you still, so it's a matter of your learning how to reach them again. You're playing catch-up with them. They've been trying to reach you since the day they died. It's also essential for parents who've lost children to reach out to other parents who understand their grief. Very few things will be more comforting than connecting with someone who's walked in your same shoes. There are others who understand what it's like to pick up the pieces of a broken heart. So please, reach out for those connections of understanding.

From my readings I've noticed that dads tend to retreat from others emotionally and hold their pain inside. I know this because the child who died often tells me this so that I can relay it to my client. It seems that dads feel like they're supposed to be able to fix anything, so they grapple with the fact that they couldn't "fix" or save their child. I think many people agree that males are taught to hold their feelings inside from a young age. But the loss of a loved one can bring overwhelming feelings. Your passed loved one can feel your pain and wants you to release it. It's not healthy to hold on to this sorrow. Sometimes all you need to release it is an understanding person to talk to who will listen and not judge you.

Dads hurt every bit as much as moms, but sometimes they aren't provided the same support system. So if you know a man who has lost a child, make an extra effort to reach out to him. Provide a shoulder for him to cry on or an ear to listen to anything that a grieving father has to say.

I've seen people distance themselves when someone dies because they don't know what to say or do for the grieving. They don't know how to make it right. Even though supporting someone who's hurting is not an easy thing to do, it's the right thing to do. To step away from people when they need you most is like kicking them when they're down. So be aware of how your actions, good or bad, can affect others. The grieving person will never forget your kindness and will never need it more than after such a great loss.

There are simple ways you can reach out and remind the grieving that you care. Bring dinner over for their family, help to clean their house, send a card to cheer them up, or phone them once a week to see how they are holding up. Any effort will mean the world to them. Try to be sensitive to their needs. Instead of asking them if they are doing well, which is unlikely, ask them if they are feeling "decent" today. That is probably the best they can hope for, for quite some time. They don't need to hear "Be strong." If you can't fall apart after losing a loved one, then when can you fall apart? Falling apart is what must happen so that you can put yourself back together again in a new form.

People who suffer a great loss will never completely be who they were before the loved one died—just as the deceased aren't exactly what they were before their death. But you know what? Just as you have to learn how to love those who've passed in a new way, they too have to learn how to reach you again. Remember, your loved ones are better than okay, and they remain here to watch you become whole again. They stay to love you and show you how fantastic they are now. They marvel at who you will become through growth and change. Make every day count, creating magic moments and stories to share with those who've passed away.

When my dad died, I was emotionally and physically maimed. I didn't want to sleep because every day that passed was a day that took me further away from the last day of his life, and it hurt. What I came to realize was that every day that carries me forward took me one day closer to the moment that my dad and I would reunite energetically. He will walk me through the thin veil that separates the living and those who live again.

Out of Sight, Not Gone

The desire for intimate connection with another person is universal. Yet the connection that is created between two people is entirely unique. When people fall in love and decide to build a life together, get married, buy a house, and have kids, they eventually develop a shorthand with each other. They can communicate with fewer words, predict each other's needs, sometimes even read each other's thoughts. This can help us during the busy times of life, when we're bogged down with who's going to wash the laundry or who's going to put away the dishes.

In readings, I find the living often end up missing the things about their spouse that they used to complain about the most. They miss their spouse's cold feet being stuck on them for warming at bedtime. Often a man misses his wife's ability to soothe him by her words and shut down his defenses with her silly "I love you" smile. These are some of the things that seem to be universal. Then there are things in readings that are completely unique, such as the deceased coming through and showing me ten boys and three girls and relaying to me that the couple have thirteen children. A husband might come through and tell me that his wife makes the best chocolate chip, blueberry pancakes in the world! Well, I think that's pretty unique in itself, but universal in that many people come through and name their favorite food and tell me they felt loved when it was made for them.

In life, we know our partner's routine, for instance that a wife is cranky in the morning without her coffee and you better not say a word until she's had it, or that when a husband has a cold, he turns into a two-year-old and needs babying. Or you might know never to give your spouse the checkbook because he or she will double up payments to pay off the balance faster, thinking he or she is doing a good thing, but end up emptying your bank account. We kiss, pout, say we're sorry, and laugh at how fast the years go by. These examples are just a drop in the bucket compared to the ocean of memories and familiarities that we experience with those we love every day. I try to remember the lessons I've learned through those who've died and those who live and miss them. When Joe rides my nerves, I take a very deep breath and I thank God for the times I've had with him and for my extraordinary daughters. I sometimes stare at Joe and the kids, memorizing every detail of their faces, and my heart swells with gratitude. Sometimes it feels like it will break, because I love them so much. It's hard for me to imagine the walls of any heart's being strong enough to contain the love that my family give me every day and the love that I have an abundance of for them. It's awfully crowded in there, and that's why God gave us hearts that were made to expand.

When a great love dies, it's devastating. There is no replacing the love of your life and your best friend. It's hard enough to fall in love and to trust someone with your deepest feelings. To hold that person in a place inside your heart that is sacred is to render yourself vulnerable. We allow ourselves to risk getting hurt because we can't imagine an end to the love that we feel. In reality, there is no end to this love. Even when we physically lose that person, the one we love has become a part of us and we are a part of him or her. The loss of a spouse or someone we love romantically is exceptionally painful. The song "The Way We Were" sung by Barbra Streisand is, I feel, a powerful telling of what losing a love can be and often is. I find this song very moving, haunting in a way. The lyrics speak of "scattered pictures" and all the happy memories from before life changed. Although the song seems to be more about losing a loved one through a breakup or divorce, you can see how the words can be applied to the death of a loved one. I know from personal experience, both from losing my dad and from seeing through the eyes of the deceased, that for pictures to be scattered around the person who is grieving is a very real occurrence that happens every day.

I've brought through many people who were and are the love of a lifetime to someone. I assure you that moving on doesn't have to mean letting go. Those who have passed still sit with you at the kitchen table, and they often sit with and touch the living loved one at bedtime, whether it's through dreams or continuing to lie on their side of the bed. Because this was their routine in life, they often continue it even after death. They do this out of love and for the comfort they feel they still bring the living. Also, the living provide comfort for those who have passed when we mention their name, talk to them directly, stare at their picture, and include them in our lives. The deceased don't exactly cry, but I have felt their heart ache for the living person they're trying to reach. It pains them to see you cry, so they will try harder to reach out to you through others, signs, or dreams until you acknowledge their presence in words or just by thinking about them—the "I know you're there" being screamed in your head and your heart.

I believe that the deceased comfort the living in many ways. Often they appear to loved ones in dreams to say they're all right. They let us "feel" their presence. They're simply reminding us that we're not alone, that they haven't left. They send us songs to communicate to us; I've talked to people who are very aware when it's a dedication being sent to them from the other side. The deceased give us all sorts of signs that they remain. People smell the perfume their mom used to wear or the cigar their granddad used to smoke. Some see orbs of light, unmistakably not of this world, appear in photographs. The deceased make toys run without batteries to say they're around the kids. They communicate through children, who lack the hang-ups that grown people have. My youngest daughter says, "Grandpa's not gone, Mom. I see him in my room. He talks to me." You get what I'm saying. They are often trying so hard to communicate that they'll try different ways to reach out to you until they are heard. Be careful not to harden your mind and heart, dismissing every sign they send you. Signs will be clear. If you keep an open mind and an open heart, you may be able to verify the presence of your loved one.

When your love story seems to end with a death, please remember that love stories never really end. That's what makes them so special. There are countless ways that we connect and communicate with our loved ones both in life and in death. Remember this: "till death do us part" doesn't apply in the afterlife. People are rejoined and whole again, and they always are where they want to be the most.

As a footnote, significant others who pass do want their loved one to be happy, and if that entails remarriage, then they're fine with that. You're not minimizing the love you have for the person who died by loving someone else for different reasons. The deceased don't sit around and watch your physical contact with other people. They are here on an emotional level to support you when you need it and advise you when you'll listen, because they know what pitfalls await you. Those who have passed have a wide view.

People often wonder which one of the men/women they loved in life will be with them after they have all passed away. This is a valid concern but one that requires no real thought or guilt. I say this because when you die, your energy seems to be emotionally based. You will be where your heart truly wants to reside. If that means around more than one person, then so be it. It's usually not, but I have had a few instances of this. I had one guy come through with three wives who had all passed before him. He seemed happy, can't imagine why. Just kidding. If a spouse dies young, then even though the living partner may remarry and live for years with another spouse, he or she often chooses to be with that first spouse. Remember, this sorting out is based on emotional energy, not thought. There tends to be unfinished business between the first couple. They often will look exactly as they did around the time of the young spouse's death. Even if a husband lived to be ninety-five, he will revert to twenty-one, if that was his age when they were parted by death. Trust me, the level of joy that I see on these spirits' faces is pure magic. This doesn't mean that a second wife from later in life is left out in the cold when she passes. The husband may choose to be with her. It depends on where he *feels* he needs to be.

Once there is no one left in the living world whom they

love, there is very little incentive for the deceased to reach the living. If there was a house, saloon, church, or other place that a deceased person spent a lot of time, he or she will sometimes remain there for comfort. For the deceased, it's not the current day; it's whatever year they were happiest in connection with the structure. This presence is sometimes referred to as a "haunting." The deceased are there usually not to hurt others but because they like being where you also happen to want to be. When there is absolutely no interest for spirits here in our world, they return to their own heaven and "live" with their loved ones who have also died.

I do, however, believe that sometimes spirits will appear back here when they are needed for intervention to save the life of a living person or to help shape a person into who he or she was meant to be by attempting to guide that person down the right path. Usually this will be a person who reminds them of themselves and whom they want to keep from walking down the wrong path—often the path that the deceased themselves had traveled.

MUSIC TO MY EARS

I learned of Allison DuBois in March of 2004. Reading news articles on the Internet, I came across one that mentioned the "Michael Jordan" of mediums. Allison had been involved in experiments at an Arizona university. The article said that she communicates with dead people. I had lost my dear husband, Bill, on 9/11/2001 at the World Trade Center. He was on the 100th floor of the North Tower, the first building to be attacked. I did not hear from Bill, and the exact circumstances of his death would be lost to me forever. Dying there was horrible, but I knew some deaths were worse than others. Some people were burned alive. Many jumped to their deaths to escape the flames and extreme heat. Of course, my imagination spun some very gruesome scenes. But when I read about Allison and the attempts of scientists to back her up, I figured this was my only chance to quench my need to know what happened to Bill.

My reading was in late August of 2004. I was very nervous. I did not want to convey any hints, to supply any information. I wanted it all to come from Bill. Allison explained that she would give me all the information that she received because she didn't want to edit anything important out. During the course of the reading, Allison asked if I wanted any specific questions answered. I said I wanted to know the circumstances of my husband's death.

She immediately said that he was in a building that was on fire. He was with other people and that he was very afraid to die and that he loved his life very much. She said that he was looking at a picture of our family before he died. Bill was just at the World Trade Center for a two-day meeting and didn't have an office there. The picture was the one that he always carried in his wallet. She said the ceiling caved in and that he "was gone" instantly. Then she said, "How is it that you don't know how your husband died?"

When I revealed his location, Allison was taken aback. Since Bill was inside the building, she couldn't see the outside. She had no idea that he was in the WTC. Information concerning other circumstances were talked about, such as information about our children, friends, and family that came through. He also talked about deceased people related to us whom he spends time around now.

When the reading was almost over, Allison said, "By the way, Bill says that when it's your turn to pass, 'We're going dancing . . . *and it's a date!*' " Before Bill's death, our local community arts center would occasionally offer ballroom dancing lessons. He was not much of a dancer, but he encouraged me to sign us up. I missed the deadline, and when the fall 2001 schedule came out, he reminded me to sign us up. I promised him I would. A week later 9/11 happened. Since his death, I would speak to him all the time. I would end our conversations by saying," And when I cross over, we're going dancing!"

What Allison shared with me that day chased away a paralysis caused by grief that had gripped my heart. I did approach her with an open mind and heart. My belief in a life after this was already a part of me, all through blind faith. Allison's reading gave me affirmation and a link with my better half that I desperately needed.

Second anniversary of 9/11:

I decided to stay home alone that day and face my sadness privately. I don't like to carry grief around 24/7 because it is such an energy drain, but I do pull it out at appropriate times, and the 9/11 date always qualifies. After watching various ceremonies on television, I decided to do some laundry. I went through some pants' pockets and found some change and laid it on the kitchen counter. I later came back to put the coins away. As I glanced down, I noticed an old wheat penny. I was thrilled because every time my husband saw one, he would joyfully point it out, saying that he would save it with other old coins that he treasured. Finding the coin and remembering made me smile. I was happy with that little sign on 9/11. But I was even happier after I picked up the coin. As I turned it over and saw the imprint of Bill's birth year, I knew that the coin was a gift. I knew that he was all around me at that moment. He was joyous, and playful, and whole. The sadness was my own, definitely not his. I liked his feelings better and spent the rest of my day with his mind-set instead of the one I had woken up with.

After my second reading with Allison on September 16, 2005:

Bill proved to Allison his skills in the kitchen by showing her his favorite food—scrambled eggs. He always enjoyed making them for the family when he was alive, especially for his beloved boxer dogs, Mike and Zelda. It was so important that Allison talked about Bill's fondness for scrambled eggs because it's specific to his personality, further letting me know he's with me. It's nice to know that cholesterol problems don't cross over with us!

Bill talked about being with relatives who had died in recent years. Allison spoke of them by name. Everyone is together. There isn't any loneliness or longing. There seems to be a sense of universal love that is private and special for each individual, yet it belongs to everyone.

Allison says that our loved ones know of our time that is yet to come, good or bad, but they understand that while we are here, we must move through, even stumble through, our humanness. And their new way of understanding is out of our realm of thinking. We will be reunited one way or another, and with the knowledge that we will someday be in their wonderful place, we should be inspired to live better lives and to make wiser choices. Allison said that Bill wanted to acknowledge the plaque that was erected in his honor. In fact, Bill's former employer had put a plaque up for Bill in the office in his honor. Allison said that Bill spoke of wanting me to take a trip and be happy. She shared details about our life together as well as things that have happened since.

I am so very happy that Allison contacted me during the fourth anniversary of 9/11. The things that she shared with me from the other side not only lessened my burden of sorrow and grief but also gave me great hope for my future, here and beyond. Every negative particle will simply fall away in an instant. Relish the spirit of those who have gone before us. There truly is no end.

Reading 9/11

When I contacted Betty about my book, I only had her name and phone number from my assistant's old records.

Having read three hundred people the year that I read her, I didn't remember that she was a 9/11 widow. I e-mailed her a few days before the fourth anniversary of 9/11. I have every confidence that Bill arranged for his wife to be read around the time of his passing. I had only sent e-mails out to five random former clients out of three hundred to see if they wanted to share their story in my book, and the only chapter that I hadn't written was "loss of spouse." She was the only one out of the five who had lost a spouse, so I'm quite sure Bill's behind this. Good job, Bill!

Betty e-mailed me back that after she returned from her trip to a 9/11 tribute, she would contact me to share the details of her reading with me. After she returned and called me, I felt compelled to reread her. The timing was right, and Bill had some things to say.

Betty called me on the day that we had agreed on for a phone reading. I told her that her husband said he sends her birds so that she knows he's around.

She shared with me that just the other day she had had a little bird fly up around her head, and she said, "I know that's you, Bill."

Sometimes birds can symbolize freedom to the deceased, a way to let the living know that they're soaring in the sky and not in the ground or in an urn. Birds are a sign of life and an expanded consciousness. Birds usually look down on us and observe us, and that's not so different from angels/spirits.

So it was nice for her to have acknowledgment from her husband that indeed this was an attempt to get her attention. They're also sort of a calling card from him, which means birds will be his way to share his presence with his wife so she doesn't dismiss him.

He shared names of family members whom he is around on the other side, names that Betty easily verified—except for one. I thought it was interesting that I kept getting the name "James." Betty said, "You kept getting that name last year, and I couldn't figure that one out."

I had a lightbulb moment. "Betty, it's a last name. Do you know someone close to your husband with the last name James?"

It then clicked in her head. She realized that Bill was talking about a friend, a Dr. James, who had also passed away. Whew! Sometimes it's harder than other times, but that was great that Bill finally got me to realize that it was a last name. Every person Bill named and said he was with was now accounted for and was someone close to his heart.

Bill also kept talking about a plaque that was for him that he loved. He wanted his wife to know how much it meant to him. It had been erected for him at his office and had his image etched onto the front.

Many pieces of information were conveyed to Betty that day from Bill, but I thought the most important was that he was thinking of her in his final moments at the World Trade Center and he still is carrying her with him. He will continue to guide and love his family as well as give them occasional urges to make his famous scrambled eggs just the way he likes them.

I would like to thank Betty for courageously sharing her story with others. Many people who lost loved ones on 9/11 will no doubt relate to her as well as empathize with her. To all of those who've loved and lost, please remember that you're blessed having loved so greatly and that love will never die.

Hurricane Katrina

In August 2005 the worst natural disaster to hit America in modern times tore through the South. Hurricane Katrina blew through Louisiana and Mississippi and left utter devastation in its wake. My friend Wendy called me distraught because her husband Jim, the news producer, had decided to head for the ruins left by Katrina. Wendy was worried about his safety, which is understandable. All I could do was reassure her. Jim thankfully returned safely a few days later.

The following week his news station held a telethon to raise money for the disaster relief fund. I called Wendy and said, "Let's go sort clothes or take food down to the coliseum in Phoenix for the evacuees. Let's do something to help!"

Wendy said, "Allison, why don't you come tonight and answer phones at the news station for the telethon?"

So that's exactly what I did. It was a great night with many ups and downs. There were pizza parlors that called in donating $4,000, there were people who offered to house an evacuee, and there were children who called in to donate the contents of their piggy banks! As I always say, much can be learned from children.

Anyway, I sat next to a nice guy named Dave, who was my age. We started chatting between phone calls. He asked me what I do for a living, so I told him, "I'm a medium."

His response was "No way!"

Then he started telling me about his friend Jason, whose wife had just died tragically. He then got on his cell phone and called Jason to tell him who was sitting next to him. All I could hear was "No way!" You can tell why those two are friends! I gave the excited friend my e-mail address, and he contacted me the next day.

Jason had lost his wife four months before our introduction. He had two daughters to take care of. My empathy was enormous, and I knew his wife orchestrated our meeting. She was taking care of him from the other side. So I told him I would bring his wife through, and I set up a reading for the following week. Jason shared that he had looked up my Web site a couple of months earlier but saw that I had a long waiting list. He had been disappointed when he wasn't able to book an appointment with me. Apparently his wife took care of this for him by cutting through the red tape and going right to the source!

Jason mentioned that he had a friend, Karla, who had

had a reading with me. Her husband had died in a car accident along with their youngest daughter and oldest daughter's best friend. He had met Karla in a support group she had founded called Safe Harbor. I immediately remembered her reading from a little over a year before. I thought, I'm going to call her because the coincidences keep adding up.

I explained to Jason what some of the information his wife might come through with would be like. I know that when I give examples to someone who is grieving, it helps the person to know what I'm actually seeing in my head. Joe, who never tires of my giving people an example, has observed that the example resonates on their faces as they begin to experience their own unique connections and realize that my example is their reality. One example that I gave Jason was "Your wife might say, I'm going to be at the little girl's birthday party."

I visualized birthday balloons held in the hand of Jason's wife, but Jason said nothing about my birthday example, so I thought I'd save it for his reading the following week. I was baffled, I must admit. The examples I give are usually very important to the deceased, so I'm used to their clicking with the living. I hung up with Jason and I called Karla to say hi.

She was quite taken aback to hear from me. As we talked, I asked her about her support group. She said it focuses on deaths involving car accidents. I asked if I could add the group's information to my Web site as a resource for others who had lost loved ones in this way, and she agreed. Karla then shared something else. Today was her daughter's birthday. She knew it was no coincidence that I called that day. We talked about how much she misses her family and that she was taking balloons to the cemetery for her daughter today. For me, this greatly reinforced the fact that we are purposely placed into people's lives when they need us the most. No doubt Karla's daughter and husband had a hand in leading me to her during this chain of "coincidences." I told Jason the next day that it was Karla's daughter's birthday. I knew that Jason's wife, Nicole, had been trying to let Karla know that she was taking care of her little girl. I knew this because when people who've passed on show me something like birthday balloons in their hand, I know they're showing a physical connection between themselves and whoever the object belongs to. A feeling of certainty that I am reading the visual correctly can also reinforce the visual that I receive. After learning of Karla's daughter's birthday, I was kicking myself for not having taken the information further, but I did share with Karla that I had mentioned the little girl's birthday to Jason. Karla knew her husband and daughter were letting her know that they saw the balloons she'd brought for her daughter and that they were with her. People who pass on find themselves connected through the relationships that the living have.

Jason and Karla have included their stories, hoping to touch others who have lost their lovers and spouses.

MRS. JASON SHERMAN

My name is Jason Sherman. My life and the lives of my family and close friends were forever changed on May 15,
2005, at 2:15 a.m., on a sad stretch of the 101 freeway in
Phoenix, Arizona. My wife, Nicole, and I had just spent the
evening with some childhood friends of hers whom she had
recently reconnected with. We had a blast! Eating, drinking,
dancing, and catching up on old times.

Her friends asked if we wanted to stay at their place
since the drive home was so far and it was so late. We decided that we should go home. There is nothing like sleeping in your own bed after a night out. Besides, later that
morning we were going to see a medium who was in town
because my wife was interested in the topic of life after
death.

On our way home, we saw what looked to be a horrific
accident in the opposite lane of traffic. The vehicles were
at a standstill. We couldn't see if anyone had been hurt.
I have an EMT license and had been trying to join various
fire departments in the valley for the last five years, so
Nicole immediately said, "Oh my God, we should pull over
and help!"

I did just that, quickly pulling over to the side of the road
that we were closest to, on the opposite side of the freeway
from the accident. It looked as though the two vehicles involved in the accident had smashed into the center dividing
cables of the median and had thrown debris all along the
freeway, even across to the other side. I jumped out and I

dialed 911 as I raced across the freeway on foot. I told them to send police and fire because it looked really bad. Just then I saw the two people in one car run away, one right past me! I asked if he was okay, and he said yeah and kept running. As I got to the median, I noticed that on their side of the freeway, there were a bunch of street racers who had pulled over. As soon as they heard the sirens, they yelled, "Cops! Let's go!" They all sped off.

Nicole had crossed with me to the other side of the street to look inside the cars to check for casualties. Meanwhile we could hear the police sirens getting closer. I told her that she should go back to the car and stay there, since it was apparent that nobody was hurt. I told her I'd finish exploring the scene and be right there. So she nodded and returned to our car. I still remember seeing her cross back over the freeway to our car and move our car more parallel to the accident.

I started to advise another person who had stopped to give assistance, letting him know nobody was hurt. We began moving debris out of the vast roadway. One car's front bumper and trim were in the lanes closest to the center on our side! Cars were still flying by us and running over debris! I thought to myself, "Man, they're going too fast. Why don't they slow down!" Just then a highway patrol vehicle pulled up on the side the cars were on. The officer got out and started assessing the scene. I had turned my back to the freeway so that I could talk to him to let him know what I had witnessed.

The next thing I knew, I heard this heavy sound of a large object hitting something solid and then the sickening sound of it hitting the ground. This was followed by the screech of a car hitting the brakes. I turned and I saw something maybe ten or so feet away from me in the lane right next to the median, which was where I was standing. I remember thinking that what I was looking at didn't look real. I actually thought that someone playing a joke had dropped a mannequin out of a vehicle. It looked very unnatural.

I heard someone say it was a body, and I turned to see people with a horrified look on their faces while they backed away. I was in the road. I turned back to look closer, thinking to myself, "No way, it's fake." That's when I noticed the clothes. They were identical to what Nicole was wearing. I felt this wave of panic and shock and sickness wash over me.

"Oh my God . . . Oh my God!"

I started to step back so that I could see into our car, which was across the freeway. I asked an officer who was out in the middle of the road to check my car. I told him that my wife was supposed to be in the car. He shined his flashlight into my vehicle . . . nothing. She was not there. By this time I had backed away from where the unnatural-looking body lay. The body dressed in Nicole's clothes.

I realized what I had been looking at all along was Nicole. She must have tried to cross back over the freeway to be with me. When I had turned to talk with the officer, she was simultaneously being hit by a car. I felt a kind of sick feeling that is beyond comparison to any other in the world, so massive I couldn't think. My head was swimming. My first thought was about our girls and how they would never see her again. How was I going to tell them? They had had no clue, as they kissed her earlier in the night at the babysitter's, that this would be their last kiss, their last time to see their mommy alive. I had no idea that as I watched her dance that night, that as she turned to me and said, "I love you," that would be the last time I would hear those words from her. No idea that as we slowly danced and held each other, an hour later she would be gone from my life.

I am forever grateful for that last dance and those last words of "I love you."

MY READING WITH ALLISON

Before I met Allison, I was in a pretty dark place. I was doing my best to get through each day. It was hard enough getting myself up to go in to work in the morning. I used to wake up to Nicole every morning and the thoughts of what the day would bring—things we had to do or were looking forward to. Now I was waking up and she was no longer next to me. My new tragic reality was the first thing I thought of upon awakening, and the last fleeting thought as I drifted off to sleep at night was of her. I was just surviving. I felt lost.

But now I had a new list of responsibilities that were solely mine. Our ten-year-old daughter, Hailey, and our seven-year-old daughter, Mckenna, were at the top of this list. I had many things to learn. I have had a shaved head for the last seven or so years. There's not a lot of thought that goes into what I'm going to do with my hair in the mornings. It is safe to say that I haven't had a lot of practice fixing the girls' hair! Ponytails, scrunchies, hair clips—forget it! I feel really bad for them. I'm trying, but they get frustrated and say, "Never mind, Dad." Does anyone know of a class to teach dads how to fix their daughters' hair? I would gladly sign up.

Losing Nicole has really made me take a hard look at my life and the things that are really important. Many times we take for granted that our partners will always be there— be there when the girls get home from school, or to go clothes shopping with them, or to fix their hair before going out anywhere. Nicole always made sure the girls looked cute. Cute hair, cute clothes. Now I'm left in charge of that—the guy who would holler out from the closet, "Honey, what should I wear when we go out tonight?"

I admit that I beat myself up because I can't do the things that she was able to do as well as she could. It's hard to accept that I might not be able to do everything and be everywhere. I feel like it's my responsibility to try to make up for their mom's not being there. I feel as if I am letting Nicole down if I can't handle everything at once—the girls, work, my feelings and emotions, cleaning the house, doing the yard. The list goes on and on. I am doing the best I can. I have to keep telling myself this.

I believe that Nicole saw me struggling and pulled some

strings to lead me to Allison. After I met Allison, I began to feel less alone. Not as lost. I'm not magically better, and I'm aware that the girls and I have a long road ahead of us. It's a start, though. Allison talked about so many things that she could not have known about except through Nicole. After the funeral, we wrote messages to Nicole on pieces of paper and attached them to balloons and let them go. Allison said, "Nicole got the balloons you sent her." My jaw just dropped. There were so many things that just blew me away.

There were some things that didn't make sense at first but did later. One in particular was a message Nicole had for her best friend, Larissa. She mentioned Larissa and showed the color purple around her—*all* around her! She also kept showing Larissa driving past a Burger King, over and over again. Nicole kept showing Allison the Burger King sign through the window of a car driving by. I know, I thought the same thing: what the heck are you talking about! About a week later, I was able to share with Larissa the things Allison brought through from Nicole. When I told her about the color purple around her, she told me how the house she just bought was entirely purple on the inside! Obviously Larissa and her husband had some painting to do before moving in. When I mentioned driving past the Burger King over and over, she said, "What day was it that you went to Allison?"

I told her that it was last Tuesday, and she got quiet. She

said that same day she went to a department store near where we live. She went over and over; she must have gone five or six times. Well, guess what's right in front of the department store. You guessed it—Burger King!

Larissa cried. She has struggled with losing Nicole like all of us have. But she has kept it pretty private. She is a firefighter, and as she does so many times in her work, she pushed aside her own fears and emotions to be there for other people. She and her husband, Jeff, were there for me and my girls from the start, and they just dove into helping me out where they could with the funeral and food and everything. Larissa is also very religious and looks to the Bible as a source of strength and guidance in her life. My reading with Allison blew her away. I think she is afraid that if she believes in it too much, it will take away or cloud her beliefs in God and heaven. But she is still so sad and lonely, as we all are early in our loss of a loved one.

What has helped me is learning that Nicole is always around us. That she is only gone in the physical sense and that she influences the girls and my life every day. This has helped to ease my sadness and loneliness. No, I can't hug her or kiss her anymore, or feel her body next to mine. But I can "feel" her presence around me if I pay close attention. I talk to her every day, telling her how much I love her and asking her to help me out when things get overwhelming with the girls. I know that when my heart lightens some more, and the anger and the guilt and the sadness lessen, she will come into my dreams again. I long for this day and

I know that we will be together again someday, when it's my time.

Medium Affected

When I met Jason for the first time, I had already written four pages of information from his wife and I was eager to share it with him. I opened the door to a friendly young man with a heavy heart. I could feel his pain. I invited him in to sit down and we began the reading.

First, I told him how amazed I was at the lengths his wife went to orchestrate a reading for the husband she still very much loves. She didn't cause a hurricane to get my attention. She did use it as an opportunity to reach me through a chain of events that were meant to happen to bring me to Jason. Spirits are very creative in setting up circumstances to get our attention. I asked his wife, "Come through loud and clear, and if there's something you want to say to your husband, now would be a good time."

Before Jason arrived, Nicole had kept showing me "her" ring around Jason's neck on a chain. I had written it down on a pad of paper. I now had my tablet of paper on my lap. As I looked at Jason, I said, "Jason, is that Nicole's ring around your neck?"

He responded yes.

"Jason, I'm going to turn my pad of paper towards you so that you know I wrote this before you got here."

I had answered the door myself with it in my hand, and

Jason knew I hadn't written anything since we'd shaken hands. He looked confused and squinted at the paper: "Jason wears wedding ring on chain because then it's close to his heart."

Jason was clearly moved, and this is important. It's why I write information before a reading. There is a heavier impact when information is received before a reading. Then no one can argue that I "saw" the necklace and inferred my information. Which is great; it removes doubt.

"Jason, Nicole keeps talking about the lock of her hair that was saved. She also keeps talking about Disneyland and your taking your girls there after her passing. So this trip is important to her, and if you didn't just take them, then you plan to. She also talks about a little boy connected to her little sister whom she's around now. She also says she 'whispers' in your ear."

Jason was busting to tell me what the information meant. I asked him to wait until I finished giving him what I had, although I understood why it was difficult to refrain.

"She's also talking about ambulance lights that were a tribute to her?" I was a little confused by that one, but it would all make sense later. "She says she got the balloons that were released to her. She says to thank the ladies that brought all of the food after her passing. She was happy that you were taken care of by the "ladies," because she would have made dinner for you in life and appreciates it that they cared so much. Don't forget to thank them for her. She keeps showing me her necklace with the heart pendant as being important to her. She says she was well liked, and she says there were a lot of females she was around who were crying for her when she passed. She acknowledges a tattoo that was created in memory of her. She says she loved Mexican food and that she's with Jack on the other side."

This is some of the information that I gave Jason that emphasized to me who Nicole is and what she's about.

Jason then came back with responses to my information. "I do hear Nicole whisper in my ear. I do have a lock of her hair that means a lot to me. I did take our girls to Disneyland after Nicole passed. She has a little sister with a small son named Cole. There was a fire engine at her funeral that turned the lights on in tribute to Nicole. We did release balloons to her. Mexican food is her absolute favorite, and my deceased grandfather's name is Jack."

Well, I did think the fire engine was an ambulance, but that's still pretty close. I was moved that Nicole kept showing herself around her nephew, whose name is Cole. Cole/Nicole—the names side by side are pretty telling. He will always be a part of her, just as he is in name.

After the reading was over, as Jason was leaving, I hoped that what I told him would help him move a tiny bit forward and help him start to heal. He'll never fully move through the loss, but he will see her again and be reunited. I was very moved by meeting Jason. I saw the similarities between me and my Joe and Jason and his Nicole. They'd been married eleven years and had two daughters. Joe and I had been married eleven years and had three daughters.

Jason said to me, "I don't understand. Nicole and I were supposed to grow old together. There were so many things we had planned on doing together."

I looked at Jason, and it resonated with me that at any moment life can throw you a curveball. I knew that from all the readings I had done and from losing my father. I was looking at a man who had married the same time I did, had children the same age that my kids are, and yet I was afforded the luxury of being able to look at my husband from across the dinner table every night. I also took in that spouses, myself included, argue over silly things, things that later we realize are unimportant. I explained to Jason that it's just life—arguing, making up and moving on. No guilt needs to exist. It's the struggles that make us strong and later cause us to either return to or reflect upon those we love.

Jason had already walked out of my house with Joe. I was still inside. Nicole whispered in my ear to go "Tell him I love him."

It seems general to some, but so what; it matters and she meant it. You bet I told him.

Nicole Sherman was planning her birthday party before she died and had picked out the band and everything. Jason and her family decided to hold the event anyway. It was the first birthday party that I ever attended for someone I brought through in a reading. As Nicole mentioned in the reading, Mexican food was her favorite, so her family catered her party from her favorite restaurant, El Charro. I also found it interesting that balloons with a note seem to be something both Karla and Jason have done for their loved ones. Both readings mentioned balloons.

In Jason's reading, Nicole had talked about wanting her two little girls to have heart necklaces. Jason explained that he had two made that had a small bit of Nicole's ashes inside the heart. He'd give them to his daughters when they are much older. Although Nicole understood why Jason was waiting, she still wanted her girls to have something right now to hold onto from her. So before the birthday party, my two younger girls and I set out in search of the perfect heart pendants for the Sherman girls. A mall on Saturday is something I only do when I absolutely have to, argghh! But brave it we did. We had been to four different jewelry stores when my second daughter, Fallon, upon entering another store, announced that this is where we would find the right necklace. She was right. We found the two perfect necklaces for the girls, and we took them to be engraved. I asked Nicole what she wanted to have inscribed on the back, and she said simply, "Mom."

Going to the party, gifts in hand, I hoped I wasn't overstepping my bounds. My girls met Nicole's. I handed one of the necklaces to Hailey, the older daughter, and she seemed happy with it. I gave Jason the necklace for the younger to be given later. My girls ran off to play as I stood and admired the cake with Nicole's young and flawless angel face on it staring back at me. I told Nicole that I was sorry that I couldn't do more for her, as I emotionally noted that I was one of many who would have liked to pull her back to our side of the veil. As my girls ran around me, I felt guilty and thankful all at the same time for being able to hug my little girls.

Sometimes after a reading with the loss of a spouse or child, I hug my family and then retreat to separate myself from them because I need to grieve privately for the deaths that hit too close to home. Sometimes I just watch my kids sleep to remember that moment forever. I "feel" for my clients that those sleeping, playing, laughing moments are the most important in life, so I remember to take in as many as humanly possible. When people die, they don't show me how much money or how many things they had. They show me the people who made them live well. It's the memories they banked that made them truly rich. I was deeply touched by Jason and Nicole's life together, and I hope their reading lets others know that there is no division of love.

After writing Jason's section for my book, I reflected on Karla and her family. I wanted to convey Karla's story in just the right way. Karla not only has experienced the loss of a spouse, which is the topic of this chapter but also lost her child at the same time. I think her story is the right one to conclude two very important and emotionally charged chapters; I hope it will add healing as well. This chapter includes three love stories that many people can relate to and admire. Karla's story is different from the other two in that she can't miss her husband without missing her daughter too, and vice versa. Karla has written a tribute for her husband that includes their love story. It's important to Karla that you feel like you know her family. She hopes her story will help others who have lost or will lose someone they love.

KARLA

The day that I received that phone call from Allison was another hard day. It was my daughter Lindsey's birthday. She would have been fourteen years old. I woke up that morning, got my older daughter off to school, and headed for the gym, thinking that was going to make me feel better. I came home, took a shower, and got dressed for the day. I remember standing in the middle of my kitchen, feeling like I wanted to go back to bed. I stood there in the kitchen crying, talking to my daughter, telling her it is another sad day. I was feeling extremely depressed. I told her I needed something to bring a smile to my face that day. Then out of the blue, I received a phone call from Allison DuBois, asking me if I would like to do a tribute to my husband and daughter. Before I could tell her it was Lindsey's birthday, Allison already knew.

Two years ago, I lost part of myself when we were driving home from a family vacation. We were approximately one hour away from home when we had a tire blow out. Our SUV rolled several times. My daughter Lindsey, age eleven, my husband, age thirty-six, and my older daughter's best friend, Tawnee Hogan, age fifteen, died at the scene of the accident. My life would never be the same. Although I can no longer see them, I am grateful for having them be a part of who I am.

To give you a little background on my husband and me, allow me to go back to where it all began for us.

I have known my husband forever, and when I say forever, I mean it. You see, our mothers were good friends at the time they were pregnant with us in Wichita, Kansas. We were born six weeks apart. I loved to tease him about being older than me. When I was five years old, my parents moved to California, and his parents moved to Colorado. When I was twelve, his father came to live with us while he found a job and a home to move his family to. I remember my mom calling me to come downstairs and meet the Whelchel boys—Brent, my future husband, and Todd. My husband told me that the moment he laid eyes upon me, he left there telling his brother Todd that I was the girl he was going to marry!

Several years passed, and although my husband tried several times to get me to be his girlfriend, it didn't happen. He was best friends with my brother, also named Brent. So, as Brent and Brent became close friends, he was like another brother in the house to me.

For our graduation, our mothers planned a party for the two of us. We talked until the early morning hours, and I realized that I was in love with Brent.

We dated for two years and were married at the young age of twenty and twenty-one. On our wedding day, Brent strolled in twenty minutes before the wedding. Time enough to raise a beer with his brothers and put on a tux. He told me surfing was great that day; the waves were too good to leave.

He was the kind of man who loved being the center of attention. Brent loved to make people laugh; he never minded others' calling him a smart-ass. (I think he enjoyed it.) He made a joke of everything; sometimes it was hard to get him to be serious. He never lost the child inside him.

His motto was "Work hard, and play hard." Brent never held back when it came to work. He looked for ways to learn and improve along the way.

Brent loved music. He played acoustic guitar and electric guitar. In the last three years of his life, he taught himself to sing, just as he had taught himself to play the guitar and drums. Brent always had a crowd cheering as he belted out songs from Stone Temple Pilots at a local sushi bar where he enjoyed karaoke. He could hear any song and immediately know the right chords to play. His love for rock and roll and playing in a band started when he was fourteen and continued until the day he died.

Brent loved to watch the Discovery channel. He especially loved anything that had to do with airplanes. So, at the age of thirty-five, he decided to take lessons to learn how to fly. He never seemed afraid of anything.

One of his brothers died almost ten years to the day before Brent died. He knew life was short, and he always told me, "Never look back. Yesterday is gone. Make the best of today, and keep your head looking forward."

It seemed as though the last few years of his life, Brent did everything he wanted to do. He took up cooking. He loved creating his own recipes and arranging his dishes on plates to make them look like they came from a gourmet restaurant. He loved serving the girls and me.

Brent was loyal to his work, family, and friends. He loved being a father, although he was a softie when it came to his girls. His light lives on in his daughter Bridget, and his music will continue to play in the hearts of all who knew him.

Brent, I will love you always and forever.

Your special Kay.

HOW I MET ALLISON DUBOIS
AND THE DETAILS FROM MY READING

During the summer of 2004 I had been working with a therapist weekly to help me through the pain that I was still feeling. My therapist had a good idea of what I believed in spiritually. So during our session, she asked me what I thought about mediums. I told her I was very open, and did she know of anyone? She told me she had seen this lady on television and had looked up her Web site. Her name was Allison DuBois. She told me that she was going to have a reading with her soon. I remember going home that day and visiting Allison's Web site. She was booked for several months, so I decided that it was not meant to be.

Toward the end of the summer I walked into my therapist's office. She looked happy and peaceful. When I told her I recognized a change in her, she smiled and told me she had had her reading with Allison. She had lost a son. Not knowing what I would say, she said she asked if she could play the first part of the tape for me. She believed my husband had come through first, to try to reach me. I believe when you lose someone suddenly, especially in a car accident, you immediately have survivor's guilt, as I did. My therapist and I were working on my survivor's guilt. The first part of the tape, Allison starts off by saying that she is seeing a young man with two very young females, one on each side of him. "He wants you to know it is not your fault. He also wants you to know that he misses sitting out by the pool and sharing a good bottle of wine with you."

None of this made sense to my therapist, but everything made perfect sense to me. Brent was with Tawnee and Lindsey, who were in the accident with him, he knew I had survivor's guilt, and he wanted me to know that it was not my fault and that he cherished our evenings in Arizona sitting out by the pool with a good bottle of wine. Allison then got through to my therapist's son, who controlled the rest of the reading. That is typical of my husband, to go after exactly what he wants.

That evening I was sitting at my computer. Out of nowhere I heard this voice that came over me, *"E-mail Allison now!"*

I went to her Web site and did just that. The next day her

assistant e-mailed me saying that she had had a cancellation, and then she clicked on my e-mail. Would I like a reading in two weeks? Absolutely!

The middle of September 2004, I went to Allison's for a
reading with my daughter. I made certain that I didn't give
her assistant any information.

Allison immediately came through with my husband.
He was standing with two very young girls, one on each side
of him. Allison's eyes filled with tears. She looked at my
daughter and me and asked, "Is this your father?"

Bridget answered, "Yes."

Allison explained that within the last week she had read
someone who had died in 9/11. She told me that she
thought the woman's husband who had passed was very
strong as he came through, and my husband was coming
through very clearly as well. This other woman turned out to
be Betty, who's also in this chapter, what a coincidence.
Allison told me and my daughter that she could feel a lot of
love among our family.

Allison continued, "This was a car accident. There was
something wrong with the tire, and the vehicle rolled."

In fact, our back left tire blew, and our SUV rolled.

Brent came through his usual way. Allison laughed because she heard Brent singing "Happy Birthday" to himself
in a comical manner. This meant a lot to me because
Brent's birthday is September 24, and Lindsey's is September 8.

Allison said, "Brent wants you know that he likes the

way he looks now. He looks better than ever." Allison also said that Brent wanted Bridget to know that the song she keeps playing over and over again in her room is the song that he sends to her, "Dance with My Father" by Luther Vandross. He wanted her to know that "although she struggles with not being able to connect with him, he sits at the end of her bed every night as she sleeps."

I had experienced several wonderful dreams of my husband, Lindsey, and Tawnee. Bridget struggled with not having dreams or signs of their being with her.

At the scene of the accident in Tonapah, Arizona, a desolate town on the outskirts of Phoenix, I was severely injured. With a severed wrist, broken bones, and contusions everywhere, I somehow managed to get myself out of my seat belt. Our vehicle was upside down. As I crawled out, Brent was seated right next to me. I kept shouting for him to wake up and help us. Allison said, "Brent wants you to remember him the way he was before the accident, not at the scene of the accident." (I struggled with this in therapy.)

I managed to get Bridget out of her seat belt—she was conscious—and to get my younger daughter's friend, who was also conscious, away from the SUV. Immediately, we had help at the scene. There were two RNs who showed up to help right away. When we finally were air evacuated to the hospital, I was rushed into surgery. I had two surgeries back to back, one on my left wrist and one on my right foot. The doctor called my sisters and their husbands and said that I had a 50 percent chance of living. I had lost a lot of blood.

At the scene of the accident, after the first roll, I remember there being a tunnel of light. My daughter Lindsey and my husband were waiting for me. The next thing I remember is their pushing me back, and the next thing I heard was my older daughter Bridget's scream for help.

Allison told me, "Brent knew that you wanted to come with them, but it was not your time. He said he knew that you would understand that he had to go be with Lindsey." After working in a hospice for seven years, every once in a while I would want to talk with Brent about what we would do if something happened to one of us. Brent always told me he did not want to talk about it, because he was "going to go first." He said he could not handle life without me.

Brent told Allison that he was sorry for not leaving me financially secure. A few months before, we had someone come out and talk to us about life insurance. With Brent's pilot lessons, our rate was very high. I had decided that we should hold off for a few more months, when our SUV would be paid off. Brent told Allison for me to never worry, he would always take care of me financially. (Funny, I have never once had to worry about money. It has always been there when I needed it.)

After the accident, I decided to do research on vehicles. I bought a Volvo. Allison told Bridget that when she starts to drive, "Your dad wants you to get a tank, an old Volvo."

Of course, this is exactly what I told Bridget she was going to get when she started driving. I have a tendency to be overprotective these days with my daughter Bridget.

Allison told us not to worry, "Brent is really watching her now!"

Allison laughed because Brent wanted Bridget to know her dad was "always watching her" and she should keep that in mind.

Over the years Brent had developed a strong relationship with his dad. He wanted us to know that he was worried about his dad, something about his heart. Not like a heart attack; he knew his dad had a broken heart.

Brent knew our anniversary was coming up soon, and he wanted me to go celebrate. He would be there with me. I had already made reservations to the Sanctuary (a project that Brent had personally worked on). He told Allison he wanted me to take a picture of him and set it at the table. He said that roses would be coming to me.

After my reading with Allison, I went home. My sister had a dozen roses waiting for me on the table. So I asked her, "Why did you get me roses?"

She replied, "I don't know. I was at the store with some flowers in my hand for you, and something made me walk back and return the flowers that I had and pick up the roses for you."

So I shared with my sister what Allison had said earlier. We both knew it was Brent.

That same week I went out to eat at the restaurant that my husband had helped build and there were roses at the table waiting for me. I don't know who sent them or where they came from, but I suspect Brent had something to do with my flowers. None of the other tables had any flowers. Bridget and I did take his pictures with us so that we would feel like he was dining with us.

Allison told Bridget and me that Brent wanted us to take a trip to Hawaii together.

Over that summer Bridget and I had talked about if we could take a trip, where would it be? Bridget told me, "I want to go to Hawaii."

I told her I didn't know if she remembered that her dad and I went to Hawaii for two weeks on our first wedding anniversary. I was seven months pregnant with her.

Allison asked if there was anyone else we wanted her to try to get through. I told her yes, my daughter. Allison immediately got Lindsey through. She told me she thought she was seven or eight. Lindsey "was very happy and playing with animals." (Lindsey loved animals.)

She said there was an older lady with her, who wore glasses. (My grandmother, I believe.)

Allison said, "She loved the balloons that she got on her birthday, and she is so touched that all her friends got together." Her last two birthdays, all her friends got together celebrating what they have made "Lindsey's Day." They bring a big cake and balloons. Together we release the balloons in front of her school, where a memorial wall and two benches sit in honor of her and her dad.

Allison said, "Lindsey was scared at first when she crossed over, but then her daddy took her hand."

Allison tells me that Lindsey says, "She lies with you at

night in your bed with her dog, Sara. She doesn't like it that you cry so much. She knows that you have the TV on, but she knows that you are not watching it." Every night, Lindsey's dog sleeps with me. I stare at the TV, unaware of what is on. I used to cry, thanking God that I had made it through another day, and wishing God would take me that night.

Lindsey wants Bridget to know "that she knows they fought like sisters do, but she loves her and there is no need for her to feel guilty." Bridget had argued with her sister two days before the accident and was having a hard time forgiving herself.

The older lady is there with her, and she is wondering if it is okay if Lindsey goes and plays now for a while.

Bridget asked Allison if she could get her best friend to come through.

Tawnee came through. She told Bridget, "She likes being there with Bridget's dad. She is worried about her mom, and for us to please watch over her." Tawnee's family has had a very difficult time.

She told Bridget that when the dogs bark for no reason, this is her talking to us. She makes them bark. The dogs still bark for no reason. Now we just tell Tawnee, "We hear you, Tawnee."

Tawnee "loves the tattoo her mom got of her. She loves the butterfly with her name on it."

Allison asked if we had any questions.

I asked why I keep having dreams of Lindsey in which

she is seven or eight, and why when Allison got her to come through, that was her age. (Lindsey was eleven when she died.)

Allison paused and answered, "Lindsey says that as she got older, things started to become more confusing to her, so when she died, she returned to the age that she was the happiest." Lindsey liked being small and babied. Somewhere between seven and eight. I have had several dreams of Lindsey in the past two years; she is always younger than she was when she died.

I enjoyed my reading and look back on it knowing my family really is still together.

For all of you who end up dealing with your own loss, the best advice that I can give you is try to connect with others who have had a similar ordeal. Although you feel all alone, there is someone out there who has more than likely gone through a very similar loss.

The Medium's Perspective

I remember meeting Karla and her daughter. Karla is a remarkable woman with a need to talk to her husband and little girl. That's what I do, so she has found the right person. I gave her reading everything I had and just hoped it was enough to ease some of the pain. I remember feeling the pain of the family, but more than that I felt the love they have for each other. As I experienced the car accident and recited the details to Karla, I reminded myself of how fragile life is.

I was astounded that Karla and Betty both had readings that were pivotal in September, and I got in touch with both of them again for my book in September. Karla's husband and daughter had September birthdays, which came out in the reading, and Betty lost her husband on September 11, 2001. So it made sense that to add their stories to this book in September would be very much a tribute to those they love. I was also struck by the coincidences that had to occur to bring Jason to me, me back to Karla and Betty. The mention of Betty, a total stranger to Karla, a year before my writing this book during Karla's reading tells me that Bill, Brent, and Lindsey already knew they were going to be a part of this book that would bring their loved ones together. The fact that I would reconnect with Karla more than a year after her reading—and through Jason Sherman and a hurricane, no less—is amazing in itself.

I think it's important to know a person's story to better understand ourselves. It's not that if you don't get a traffic ticket in your whole life, you go to a better place than everyone else. It's not that anyone who has suffered a loss could have prevented the passing if they had prayed harder or made a deal with God to stop it. I tried that one myself. It didn't work; my dad still passed. Karla "gets" what her life with Brent was, and she didn't take it for granted. She emotionally drank it in and now lovingly recounts her life with him. I remember when I "read" Karla as she was trying to process her enormous loss. She wasn't mourning the love of her life singularly—that's unimaginable by itself—she also was grieving losing her baby, Lindsey, and her daughter's best friend.

I reflect on how I see people pick themselves up after such great loss time and time again, and I'm in awe. I see them fueled by the love they still have for the loved ones who exited too early. People who live well ultimately die well too. By this I mean, they leave people who know how strong the love exchanged is, and they know that it remains. When you take the time to show others that they matter to you and live life large, you become a person whom others learn from. Others then look at their own life and remember to make it count.

This is not to say that you have to live a flawless life. My dad, for example, would have taken back some of the decisions he made. When I sat with him before he died, he apologized for not attending my wedding because of a falling-out he had with my family. Because he said this to me in life, as much as I'd love to have that day back to spend with him, I have no more pain in my heart about my wedding day. He removed that simply by saying he was sorry and that he'd do it differently now. His apology came at my aunt Olivia's funeral. Following the apology, my dad said, "You never know when the next funeral will be your own."

And it was—his own.

See how easy it is to live and die well. My dad fixed something that bothered me in life that would have gnawed at me even more after his death. He lived well because he put his ego aside and asked for forgiveness. Usually all it takes is an "I'm sorry" when you love somebody.

Brent loves Karla and she knows that, and she knows he's still with her. Brent spent his life wisely. You can see by what Karla wrote in tribute to Brent that he did it right. Learn your lessons in life, love while you're here, swallow your pride. Love yourself enough to allow others entry to love you too. Five minutes after finishing Karla's section, I walked outside and a *huge* butterfly circled my head. My eight-year-old said, "Mommy! Look at the butterfly. It landed on your head."

Joe confirmed the size of it, and I sat back reflecting on the call that I had just received from Karla half an hour before my brush with the beautiful butterfly. Karla had spoken of the bird and the huge butterfly that had fluttered very close to her as she chronicled her contribution to the book. She knew they were sent to her from her family. Personally, I think the butterfly was her daughter. The bird, I think, was her beloved. That's just my impression. Karla would know best.

Medium

I included this chapter for all of the fans of *Medium*. I am often asked, "Did that really happen?"

Meaning, did what happens in the episodes happen in my real life? The answer is it depends on which episode you're talking about.

First, I want to thank all the *Medium* fans for giving us such a warm reception. I've heard from thousands of you who can relate to my character Allison, Joe, and their girls. I appreciate and can relate to your feeling that you are finally seeing that you belong. I also hear from many of you who have lost someone you love, and you express how nice it is just to know those who have passed remain with you.

I've included some of the many episodes that I'm asked about from the first season of *Medium*. I hope this scratches an itch for all of the inquisitive ones out there.

I can understand the curiosity around shows based on real people and the desire to know how much of the show parallels the life of the real person. I think both the show and my books are resources that many people can relate to, since we've all felt to some extent misunderstood for, even burdened by, who we are. The show has the benefit of outstanding writers who successfully capture the world as seen through my family's eyes. And even though our family seems unique, we actually face a lot of the same problems that any family does.

Most of the episodes do have at least one story line that is true to my life. Sometimes this is the family relationship story, rather than the investigation. Such as Joe tries to surprise me with a trip for my birthday, and I reach under the bed and pull out a suitcase already packed. Joe can never surprise me with a gift because I already know what it is, and usually how much it cost. There are thirteen years of these instances that the show could draw from and that I could share with you, so I'll share a recent one. In September 2005 we were going to the Emmys. Joe bought me a beautiful ring to surprise me. I looked at him and rattled off the cost of the ring to the exact penny, which made Joe's jaw drop. He jokingly said, "Get out of my head, Allison!"

It is possible for me to be surprised as long as he doesn't say to me, "You'll never guess what I got you."

That only starts my mind wandering, which results in an object's popping into my head. Many people who can predict future events hear motives and thoughts from others, which results in a picture of the object in question popping into our heads. So I told Joe a long time ago, "If you don't bring it up, I can usually ignore images of your surprises popping into my psyche."

He's had to learn how to be married to someone he can't hide gifts from in a closet or under a bed. Unlike most husbands, he has to worry about hiding them from me in his head. When I touched the ring and knew exactly how much it cost, even I was amused with myself. I thought his surprise was pretty great and he did a good job keeping it from me, except that I spent a couple of weeks feeling deception around him. To me, deception feels like when you know you are telling a lie or you're leaving something out and you feel like everyone's staring at you because they don't believe you. For me, that feeling is followed by my face getting warm. When I'm being deceived, I experience the same feelings as if I myself were doing the deceiving. It's the senses in my body giving me the forecast. I was happy when he gave me the ring, because the deception feeling went away. Whew! Lucky for him, I was preoccupied writing this book, so I didn't let these feelings make me hell-bent on getting to the bottom of his secret.

This past Christmas Joe again made the mistake of saying, "You'll never guess what I got you." He said that he figured that if he waited until the last minute to decide on and buy my present, there wouldn't be a picture in his head for me to see. So when he asked the question I couldn't stop myself. I smiled, ran toward him, and jumped into his arms.

"You got me a frozen margarita machine! I can't wait to have my friends over."

I looked up and I saw Joe's face fall. I felt bad and said, "I'm sorry, Joe."

He looked down at me and smiled. "I'm glad you like your present. I know that you like to entertain. Besides, you were surprised when you saw the picture in my head."

That's true. After all, I am surprised one way or another, so I do get the same initial rush of excitement that everybody gets. Joe is relentless in his efforts to surprise me, and I'm always looking forward to what he'll think of next. Maybe next time I'll have a better poker face and look surprised.

When you watch *Medium,* sit back and enjoy a great television program knowing that I'm watching it with you.

Like Glenn Caron, the creator of the show, says both in play and truth, "Allison, the wheels of justice turn slowly, and you can't work cases fast enough to fill all the episodes."

Not all the cases on the show are cases I've worked, but it's not the cases themselves that are important to the story line of the show but the way they affect my character and the family. One of the most important facets of *Medium* is how it shows a family learning to deal with what comes their way and how they become closer and stronger for it.

Just the Facts

In the opening episode of *Medium* I am an intern at the district attorney's office. That is in fact true; I interned in my graduating semester at Arizona State University, where I met the man I respectfully refer to as "Chief," who's wonderfully portrayed by Miguel Sandoval. Glenn has met the real DA, and they seemed to both think a lot of each other. I think a lot of them both too.

One of my jobs as an intern was to sort the crime scene photos, and while doing so, I noticed that I could see flashes of what happened before the victim in the photo was killed. I could also see details around the killer, such as a name, cars, accomplices, motive, and other details. It was unnerving, and I wasn't sure what to make of what I was seeing. I mean, I had seen things that had happened in my life in the form of flashes of pictures in my head, but I guess because I had never been exposed to actual crime scene photos, this flash of images all seemed new to me. I toyed with the idea that maybe I was an overworked mother of three girls who needed a break. This seemed plausible but still didn't fully explain what was happening to me. I wasn't even sure that I wanted to explore the possibility that I was seeing flashes of the actual violent crime. The first episode of *Medium* is a very real depiction of what happened in my real life.

I am actually married to an aerospace engineer (rocket scientist) named Joe. We challenge each other intellectually, and we can be very playful with each other. The relationship on the screen is very "us." It's strange to have a portrayal of our relationship out there to be critiqued. I wouldn't change the way Joe and I are together; it works for us. People who know us constantly comment on how much the relationship in the show is similar to our real-life relationship. We also have three fantastic little girls who share my gift, a gift that I believe is genetic.

While I was interning, I told Joe what was happening to me. We thought it might help to test the theory to see if I was just "seeing things" or if it was something far bigger than that. So I chose three random murder/missing cases and created "write-ups," which is my term for writing down any information that comes to me that is connected to the victim. There was a large part of me that wanted to prove that I wasn't doing what I thought I was doing. We faxed these write-ups to law enforcement across the country, expecting to hear nothing. To my surprise, I was contacted by the Tarrant County Sheriff's Office in conjunction with the Texas Rangers. After a couple of phone conversations with them, I decided to go out there to see if I could help in any way. I still wasn't quite sure how this all worked. I wasn't sure how to read all the signs or if I was even supposed to be a part of this case at all. I nervously and hesitantly headed to Dallas. The law enforcement officials picked me up at the airport, not at a private airstrip as in the show. I wish!

They did take me to areas that the victim had "potentially" been taken to testing me. I then said to the officer, "He did not bring the child here."

A few minutes later the officer acknowledged knowing that already, because scent dogs had been brought through those areas before my visit. At the time I was a little miffed by this treatment, but it was naïve of me to think that I wouldn't be tested by the police. Still, we didn't have much time before the sun would go down, and I wanted to cover as much territory as I could. Their tests were wasting my time. Then again, it was my first case, so I was unsure exactly what it was that I was expected to do or what I should expect from law enforcement. It was frustrating, frightening, and exhilarating all at the same time. In the five and a half years since my first write-up, and thousands of people's personal tests later, I've come to understand it's human nature to challenge others. I now try not to take it personally.

I did tell the sheriff that the perpetrator had shared his information with the guy in the next cell, which was also acknowledged by the police to have occurred but could not be used in court. Unfortunately, my information alone can't fix injustices. We have to work within the confines of the law. We also have to have the support of a higher power, which can have a bigger plan that we can't always see the full scope of. We don't always know how someone's life is supposed to be changed by a serious set of events.

The real sheriff from the story line of the first episode did indeed have a heart problem that I talked to him about when he said, "Tell me something about me."

The female officer in the car burst out laughing when I shared that I picked up on a physical defect with his heart that would need surgery and serious treatment. Apparently the sheriff had had heart surgery just shortly before my visit. Unfortunately, he had another heart attack after I left. You may recognize some of these details from the first episode.

There indeed was a Hurricane Alison that came through before it was arranged to have scent dogs taken out. I did throw a temper tantrum when I got home, not being able to understand what good my abilities are if I couldn't produce the Texan child's remains. I also struggled with hearing Joe's thoughts and feeling that he didn't fully believe me and didn't know what to think of me. I would look into his eyes, and his eyes looked uncertain of me, which was painful for me, since I had never seen this look before. I could hear his thoughts, questioning what to say to me, how to choose his words carefully so as to not offend me. Our real-life experience over this incident was very much like that in the first episode of *Medium,* where our characters have words over whether or not Joe believes Allison and he doubts her claims of what she "sees."

In August of 2001 I flew to Dallas to be met by officers from the sheriff's department of the county where the missing child lived when she was abducted. I was also met at the airport by a couple of cars full of Texas Rangers. We shared a lovely lunch together at a local Chinese restaurant. I have never felt as safe as I did having ten to twelve Rangers, sheriffs, and police officers with me at 7-Eleven while I purchased a Big Gulp. It was very intimidating at times, absorbing that I was in the company of such authority as I struggled with understanding my visions as well as wondering how the hell I had gotten myself into this situation.

One brave officer actually was kind enough and secure enough to go on the record for me in 2002 when channel 12 news in Phoenix ran a story on me and some of the cases that I've profiled locally in Maricopa County. The sergeant issued a public statement for channel 12, saying that he worked with me on this particular missing child's case and that I provided information on the case that "impressed" him. I provided information that had never been released publicly, such as accomplices and multiple vehicles used in the crime. Since it's a matter of public record, meaning his name was run on the evening news, I feel comfortable publicly thanking Sergeant Bobby Atteberry. Bobby was the person who first told me about the Amber Alert, which I hadn't heard of until that day. I don't think he realizes how many Arizona children he helped by sharing his emotional recollection of the death of Amber Hagerman (abducted and murdered in Texas), the child who inspired the Amber Alert. I spoke of initiating this system for Arizona in my book *Don't Kiss Them Good-Bye*. I was able to initiate the program and serve on the task force to design it. Thank you, Bobby. Meeting you was a pivotal moment in my life that I will never forget.

One of the many Rangers who picked me up at the airport that day and who was willing to take a chance on my information was Ranger Ted Poling. He was a genuinely nice man who clearly took the abducted girl's case personally. She affected every officer I came in contact with that day so intensely that I'm sure at the end of the day they all took her home with them in their heart. I know I did. I think officers who use valid psychic profilers should be applauded for putting the victim first and ignoring naysayers who, in truth, can't bring them any closer to resolving their case.

I think anyone with good sense can understand why I tend to avoid broadcasting the names of law enforcement officials whom I work with, since clearly I have to make sure these fine people aren't harassed by skeptics with too much time on their hands.

The way I look at it is, I'll keep working cases, reading people, and helping when I can, while others argue about whether or not it's possible.

Medium, Extra-Small

In another episode of *Medium,* my middle daughter, Fallon, regularly talks to "an imaginary friend" who turns out to be a child who died. This was true. She did experience this. In reality, her "imaginary" friend was a little girl who had passed away. Fallon was four when this happened and now, four years later, she still occasionally brings her up. My daughter used to make us set a place at the table for her unusual friend, and being who we are, we did! On *Medium* she met the deceased child on the playground; our little girl

acquired her "imaginary" friend in her preschool class-
room.

She also had trouble making other friends because she
was too busy playing with her "imaginary" friend, so Joe
and I set out to make an effort to expand her social calen-
dar. You may remember that our characters on the show do
the same. It wasn't easy for us, because our daughter definitely lives in her own world, and of my three daughters, she
is the quirky one, but I really love and appreciate that about
her. She has since found friends who are little mediums
themselves or are simply unique kids too.

This is one of my favorite episodes. I like it because it
shows nonmediums what the children who are mediums go
through trying to understand why everyone doesn't see
what they see. It was also like scratching an itch for me, because when I was a child, I didn't have anyone to guide me
through the growing pains of being a young medium. This
episode of *Medium* will continue to open many eyes and
hopefully resonate with the young.

All of my daughters' personalities portrayed in the show
are accurate. My oldest daughter, Aurora, whose character
is named Ariel on the show, is very much an eldest child.
She's a go-getter. She's well liked. She's used to winning.
She doesn't know her limitations yet because she's so busy
giving it her all in whatever sport she's in. Aurora's made a
sport out of picking on her little sister Fallon, which we're
trying to break her of, as on the show. She's also inherited

her father's math ability—very much as on the show, except it turns out on the show that her math aptitude comes from her pulling the answers out of my husband's head. In reality, she really is advanced in math. Her father has bragging rights there.

My middle daughter, Fallon, is an exceptional little singer, a very vocal little girl and very wise for such a little kid. When Fallon was four years old, Joe and I had the girls outside looking at the stars. Fallon looked at the moon and said, "Look, it's a new moon!" Joe looked at me and said, "Allison, you can see just a sliver, it is a new moon." She never ceases to amaze us. She's also very generous. When she was in the second grade, her school was collecting money to clothe and feed an orphan. Fallon came home at high speed, went straight to her "hidden" tooth fairy money, collected it up, and asked us if it was okay for her to give it to the school for the orphan. You can tell what your child is made of from a pretty young age. I must admit, she makes me proud and grateful to be her mom. Joe and I gave her a little extra money to take in and she was elated. Fallon mixes her food together and makes animal figurines out of her mashed potatoes. She is stubborn yet sensitive and one of the most comedic kids I've ever seen. What makes it more funny is that she's not trying to be funny, she just is.

Sophia is my baby. Everybody just adores her because she's tiny and bubbly, and she reminds me a lot of my dad. She's a natural little dancer who loves to play dress-up. Her bedroom looks like a fairy tale. Her ceiling is painted to look like the sky. While tucking her in one night, I said, "Look, honey, it looks like heaven." She whispered to me, "Mommy, I think I can see the angels." She melts me on a regular basis, and although the character inspired by her on the show is still very young, she gives you a glimpse at what a doll my little one is. They're both pretty far up there on the cute meter.

As my daughters begin to experience their gift, I walk them through their various senses and I explain how to "read" what they see and hear as little mediums. It really is special to me to be able to be their guide through life and to share in their excitement when they one-up their mom through a great prediction.

My husband, Joe, is a brilliant aerospace engineer who has recently retired for obvious reasons. He's tall, handsome, and sarcastic. On the show *Medium,* Jake Weber does a fantastic job portraying my Joe. It is true that Joe dotes on his little girls. He is usually the only person who can talk sense to me, and he defuses my cranky moods with his sarcasm and humor just as on the show. I think he may have raised the bar a little for husbands around the world, not bad. Unlike in the show, I don't wake up screaming all that often, and in reality my Joe's a much heavier sleeper than his character on the show. He's also working on developing that wonderful "six-pack" that Jake Weber sports on the show in his abdominal area. The real Joe isn't quite there yet, but no worries, he makes up for it in his infectious laugh and his immeasurable patience.

Oh Brother!

The episode of *Medium* called "Lucky" shows my brother Michael and his struggle with trying to both understand and ignore his ability to see and hear those who've died. He was in the army and went to war, where he used his instinct to return home to us in one piece. That is all true to my real brother Michael. In real life, he's older than me by five years. He's not my younger brother, as in the show. Also, my brother is much more intelligent than his character and wouldn't put up with bullying from anybody! He is, however, proud and, in the end, does the right thing, as the character demonstrates. He also is not a fan of X-rated movies as in the episode of *Medium,* but he does like the ladies.

My real brother Michael grapples with his abilities. He sees images, but hearing those passed is something he still works on. He can hear them talking but can't always make out the words being said. I can imagine how frustrating that must be. He also knows when things are going to happen before the fact. He has a great sense of danger, as well as a great instinct concerning people and their motives, which helped to bring him back to us from a war that killed some of the men who were ranked above him in his group. He's very brave and can be very modest. This episode was difficult for me to watch. It's hard to see right before my eyes the pain and confusion that exists in mediums, including my brother, whom I love dearly. Sometimes we talk about what we see and hear from the other side, and I think we help each other. We can joke medium to medium. This ability is not an easy thing to talk to just anyone about. Also, having it doesn't obligate you to make a career out of it. Sometimes just trying to understand it is enough.

As in the episode "Lucky," I did work a case where I was asked to sit in front of a house that was severely burned and write my impressions down for the DA's office. I told them that I saw that a woman was murdered. I told them what room she was murdered in and who committed the crime. It was very difficult to sit in my car writing down what I saw and what the victim was telling me. Now, in the episode "Lucky," the victim was a child. In real life, the victim was a grown woman and the perpetrator was a different family member. These are the sort of details that are changed for the show's story lines in order to protect the surviving loved ones of the deceased. It's never easy to fathom that a person could take the life of another without remorse, but unfortunately it happens all the time. That episode from *Medium*'s first season is hard to watch for me but still remains one of my favorites. Oh, and in the episode my brother's friend kills their commander. I'm sure that you can guess that didn't happen in my real life, but that's a good thing.

Like Mother, Like Daughter

There was an episode of *Medium* where my eldest daughter, "Ariel," worked a murder case with me that involved a young girl. This happened in reality, although I hadn't shared that with the writers of *Medium,* so that episode semi-paralleling my life was just an eerie coincidence. In reality, I wrote the first name of the missing girl on a piece of paper and gave it to my daughter, telling her to just write down whatever she saw or felt. I really wasn't expecting anything from her, but I wanted to see if she could profile.

I was stunned when she handed the paper back to me with a profile of the perpetrator similar to mine. She looked at me and said, "Mom, it felt like I was guessing."

This is a term little mediums use because details pop into their head and it can seem too easy to receive information. I explained this to her and told her how well she did. I had never shared anything about any missing cases with her. In fact, I had just spent the weekend with Laurie Campbell and Janet Mayer, who are also profilers. I wrote the same name on a piece of paper for each of them. We spent less than an hour on our write-ups. We then took turns reading what we had received. Many pieces of information overlapped, and some added different information, great clues. We then shared our information with the detective who had requested it. The interesting thing with my oldest daughter is that she drew diagrams of the street that the perpetrator lived on that coincided with our own drawings. Not every profiler draws diagrams. I do, and apparently so does she. She also got the correct description of the suspect's vehicle, misspelling the make of the vehicle, which just reminded me how young she really is.

Aurora didn't see any grim details because she doesn't have a reference in her head for some of the things that older mediums/profilers see, thank God. I couldn't allow her to profile otherwise, because I couldn't subject her to that. I know that one day that will change and she will have references in her head to compare her feelings and impressions to. Nonetheless, I was proud of her and impressed with her abilities. I saved her first write-up for her scrapbook. That's one of many ways that my family is different from some others. Not good, not bad, just different.

My daughter still talks to the murdered girl and passes messages to me. She feels friendship connections with those who've passed, just as I do. Once you've emotionally connected to a person who's passed on, you feel like you know them and still think about them from time to time. Sometimes they'll return to you when something's up with the living person you read when you brought the deceased through. You feel especially close to the deceased who died traumatically because they're sharing information about their death, and that's pretty personal stuff.

In the episode of *Medium* in which my character works with her daughter to get a wider assortment of information, the missing girl was still alive. In reality, unfortunately, our missing girl is deceased. Of course this means that we did not charge up to the house and save the living girl. In real life, I have devoted many hours to trying to move this case forward, and I believe I've helped to do that. Recently we've pinpointed an incarcerated suspect who needs to be cracked, a work in progress. I just want to bring the girl home to be buried and make sure the guys responsible can't hurt anyone else.

"Mother-in-Law"

This episode was particularly important to my husband, Joe, since it dealt with his mother and the loss of his father.

I enjoyed that this episode illustrated what many women already know, which is what a mother-in-law can be like. In this episode, my mother-in-law, played by Kathy Baker (whom I loved in *Picket Fences*), was widowed. My real-life mother-in-law is widowed as well. I think Glenn Caron beautifully showed the regret that my father-in-law had when he died and he saw the mistakes that he'd made, including not being there enough emotionally for his wife. My real-life mother-in-law married Joe's dad when she was nineteen. He passed away from cancer when she was around fifty-eight years old. My father-in-law, as I described him to Glenn, was a tough bird. He was very intellectual (an MIT grad). He was also not terribly emotionally available to his family, but he loved his family very much. He indeed enjoyed smoking cigars, as illustrated in this episode.

My real father-in-law does spend a great deal of time around Joe's mom since his death, and I formed a relationship with him at his insistence. I met him after he died, not before. He was never shy about telling me how I could do things better. But I'm sure that when I had to pass my math class to graduate from college and I asked him to "help" me, he was the one who showed me the answers so that I could graduate. I only squeaked by in college math; I am not mathematically inclined. He also came through and gave me information for Joe's mom, including an apology with information that was something only he'd known. That rattled her because it involved her keeping a secret and he spoiled it for her. Jim has a wicked sense of humor; I like that about him.

Joe's mom did enjoy coming over and sharing with me her wisdom concerning homemaking, and I'm quite sure that she's had moments when she thought I wasn't doing a chore, like making dinner, efficiently enough or with the right ingredients. I don't think she's unlike other mothers-in-law that way; they mean well. We all love her. It was very significant for Joe to be able to watch this episode of *Medium* and feel some comfort, seeing a scenario unfold on the screen that I had described to him years before when I brought his dad through.

Not an Exact Science

I can't break down every episode of *Medium* because it would take forever. Please keep in mind that *Medium* is inspired by my life but not a biography of my life. There will be some episodes that are just great writing and nothing more. One episode that comes to mind is the one about a professor named Dr. Caldwell, who thinks that his brother died only to find out many years later that he's still alive. This is a fictitious character, not based on a real person. Yes, it's true that I was studied by real scientists in a university lab, but Dr. Caldwell is just a character created by Glenn Caron and his fantastic staff of writers. The real scientists whom I have worked with are not like Dr. Caldwell in any way, and they will not be characters on the show.

I have worked many cases where the missing person was thought to be deceased and was in reality alive. I live for these cases, because they show that there are happy endings out there in the world. So the real similarity, I guess, is that I've worked other cases with the same happy outcome, but that's it. I've never been studied by a scientist who specializes in sleep disorders, but I can understand why Allison (the character on *Medium*) would be a candidate for that kind of study. I'm glad that so many people enjoyed this episode, and I'm sure Glenn will keep you all guessing which characters are real and which are his creations.

To all of the fans of *Medium,* thank you for watching and thank you for sharing my life.

CHAPTER 4

Living with Gifts

All people with intuitive gifts must learn how to comprehend signs. The best way for me to illustrate how a medium/predictor learns is by using myself as an example. For all of you with your own stories of predicting people's death, picking up on vibes that others put out, and other intuitive gifts, this chapter will reassure you that you're not alone. I get many letters from people who find solace in knowing that, although they thought they were isolated in their gift, they are in truth a part of a far bigger family. My dad always said, "Make no apologies for who you are." For those of you who feel overly responsible for everything around you and even burdened by your awareness and your abilities, I have a suggestion. Try writing "Make no apologies for who you are!" on your mirror or somewhere that you will see it when you wake up in the morning. This will serve as a reminder to deflect any shame that you have owing to others' closed minds.

Any saying/mantra that inspires you is worth recognizing regularly and taking in so frequently that it becomes a part of who you are. For the longest time I had "Go to your destiny!" written in lipstick on my bedroom mirror. I heard it for the first time on *Oprah* when two Olympic runners who came from a troubled neighborhood explained how they beat the odds and emerged as successful people from a place where most people didn't emerge at all. They inspired me to live by those words. Instead of hesitantly climbing out of bed, wondering what obstacles I would face, I sprang out of bed ready to "Go to my destiny," whatever that might be.

There is nothing to be ashamed of in just being who you are. As a matter of fact, you should feel blessed to be given the ability to connect with others in such a profound way. Instead of saying, "It's a curse to know when someone is going to pass ahead of time," try, "How fortunate am I to be given the opportunity to say good-bye to someone I love and sometimes even to allow myself to be used as an instrument to help save someone's life."

For those people who share your gifts in other ways, like being the nurse with unbeatable bedside manner most of us pray for when our loved ones are in need, know that your gifts are just as great. You might be the grocer the elderly look forward to seeing every week because you brighten their day. There are so many gifts that a person can have. What they all have in common is that only sharing your gift with others makes it meaningful. Mediums/predictors can share our gifts in ways that aren't overstepping our bounds. We can listen to those who need to talk and mix in a little of our intuition with good advice for a person who needs a friend. There's a time and a place for everything, and as with any gift, sharing it is only helpful when it's welcome.

Living well is partially about perspective, and then action. If you have a moment of inspiration about how you might improve the quality of another person's life and don't act on it, then you've really done nothing with that inspiring idea. So know you're being guided, and take that next step. Not only will you be helping another, but by helping that person, you will find the true definition of who you are, one that was written long ago but is being looked at for the first time.

Can You Feel It?

I urge you to pay attention to what is around you. I think many of you experience a heightened sense on a daily basis. It's nothing that will be outwardly validated: you won't be born with a special birthmark; no Red Sea will part for you. It's a human ability that you can learn to rely on and trust completely. You must be validated from within, not by others. I find that as human beings, we often doubt ourselves and punish ourselves for things that are beyond our control. This chapter illustrates the importance of trusting your instincts and encourages those who sense presences not to deny their existence.

For those of you who "feel" as though someone is standing behind you, or "feel" as though someone is standing at the foot of your bed, or even sitting on it, for that matter, I hope this chapter will speak to you. You aren't imagining a presence. In fact, you are a sensitive being with the ability to "feel" on a grand scale. I will try to guide you through understanding your special sense.

Some people reading this chapter who may be able to sense illness need to learn more about what they feel. In my first book, *Don't Kiss Them Good-Bye,* I talked about being six years old when I had my first spiritual encounter: my great-granddad appeared at the foot of my bed after his funeral. I described feeling "on edge." Part of what I meant by that has to do with sensing illness. My great-granddad had passed from intestinal cancer, which is not such a nice way to pass. I felt sick to my stomach and had an almost static-electrical sensation on the surface of my skin. Once I became an adult medium, I learned to recognize that feeling as something that would occur only when I was in the presence of someone with cancer. When I bring a person through who is dead, the deceased makes me feel something physical connected to the cause of death, almost like a calling card to identify who it is for the living. This doesn't mean that the dead are still in pain; they're not. It's just a way for them to communicate who they are to us.

I also realized that I would have the same feeling when I was in the presence of a living person with a specific disease, such as cancer. Some people don't know why they sense something that they can't explain or define, like illness or deception around a person. Many people in the health professions may have a special knack for this sense, partially from being exposed to illnesses over and over, and they learn to trust different feelings for various sicknesses. We are all individuals, so we may sense things in different ways. What feels like a heart attack to me may feel like something else to another intuitive person. I'll share what it feels like for me. Perhaps it's the same for many others. If your feeling is different from mine, it doesn't mean you're wrong, it just means that the same information is coming to you in a different way. When I sense a heart attack in someone who is living, it feels different from the heart attack of someone who has already died. In the presence of someone who died of a heart attack, I feel like I've had a small punch to the chest. It takes my breath away a little bit. That's how the dead communicate the cause of their passing to me.

If you experience these feelings and they're too much for you, acknowledge to the person passed that you understand the cause of his or her passing and ask the deceased person to ease up on that message. The deceased are fine with that and just need to be reminded sometimes that they are coming through loud and clear. They need to know that they can use less energy because they are being "felt" by the living. You can imagine how frustrating it is for them to not be heard after their death. They learn to turn up their energy as loud as they can as they walk through a room full of people with ear plugs/blinders until they find someone who doesn't have ear plugs/blinders. Imagine their relief. Once acknowledged, they will turn down their volume if you ask them to. If you have a loved one who passed away who does this to you, tell the person you're glad he or she is here and you'd love to have his or her love and guidance in your life. This will remove the feeling of frustration or aggravation that you might be feeling from the person. All the deceased want is to be acknowledged and accepted.

When I feel heart trauma around the living, it comes in different levels of seriousness. The least serious is when someone will need heart medication. I see this and hear "treatable." Sometimes I'll feel a heartburn sensation and will visualize it as being in the chest, but I sense that the damage isn't yet severe and can be treated through diet and minor medication. In other words, it's not taking the person's life anytime soon but could become more severe, so I recommend seeking medical attention. Sometimes it's the beginning stages of a blockage in an artery or plaque forming, something that's just beginning. Also, I tell people to be persistent and make sure they find a doctor they feel comfortable with. Never second-guess your own sense, most especially when it has to do with your health or the health of someone you love.

On occasion, when it's a more severe heart problem, I literally see surgery in the future or the living person standing in a hospital gown, but I also sense a "fixability" around their heart, as if he or she is not going to die right now from it but still has time. Intervention is possible at this point because the damage is not so severe.

The most severe level of heart disease I experienced with my own father. I would hug him good-bye, and when he pressed against me, his chest felt heavy to me, as if his heart wasn't beating—which in that moment made letting go of him nearly impossible. His energy felt like it was nearly gone, which meant to me that the life he still contained was very little and would soon run out. Sadly it did. There is also a sense that I get when anyone's days are short. It feels like the person's story has come to an end and there's no more left to "read." It's like reading a good book and knowing you're close to the last page and feeling disappointed there's no more to enjoy. You close the cover of your book and feel puzzled, wondering what other exciting things might happen if the book could just last a little bit longer.

After you do what I do for a while, you learn to gauge how long a person has to live by the level of energy that you feel the person still carries. There are pros and cons to this ability. On the one hand, you know when you need to say and do all the things that will matter to you and the person who will pass away. On the other hand, you're saying good-bye every time you see or talk to that person, and you don't have the luxury of thinking that everything is just fine. I spoke of this in my first book, *Don't Kiss Them Good-Bye,* when I shared the prediction of my own father's death and my inability to stop it from happening. Two years of sending him to heart specialists just wasn't enough. Oddly, they all said that his heart was fine, but it wasn't. When somebody's time is up, it's up, and, for whatever reason, only some predictions can be affected by intervention. I've told many clients of pitfalls that I see before them, such as a car accident, or I suggest that they get their chest X-rayed. It seems that I can touch most events in a positive way, but there are also some that cannot be stopped. I try to remember to have faith that things happen the way they're supposed to, but I'm only human. The way I look at it is the grass is always greener on the other side of the fence, and you just have to enjoy your own landscape.

On the television show *Medium,* the character Allison DuBois sees bad things before they happen, and sometimes she intervenes in time and sometimes she doesn't. She often finds out that her vision was part of a bigger picture, that the victim was not to be saved. My life is no different.

The only people who read signs are the ones intuitive enough to acknowledge them as signs and to accept them as a form of communication from the unseen to us. Signs, sent by relatives or friends who've passed, come in many forms. They are sent to us because those who have passed are trying to guide us through life. I asked for a sign when I was deciding whether to be a medium professionally or to go through law school. I didn't get the answer at the time that I had hoped for, but we can all see that I am where I'm supposed to be. After I asked for a sign—and this is where you have to be careful what you ask for—I received numerous signs. While driving I took a wrong turn and ended up behind a car with a license plate that said "Oracle." Another said "Medium." Then I passed a sign that said "Oracle" and ended up on a street called Campbell, which is the last name of another medium who was studied in the laboratory with me and whom I've now come to know very well. That's how it started. Then so many signs were thrown my way that I never actually caught my breath again, and now I'm here where I belong. It was frustrating though. I sent out all my law school applications after triple-checking each one. I sent them several months in advance. Two days before the deadline I received every application back in the mail. Each one had a note that said, "You're missing something," then each went on to identify an item that was checked off on my checklist but that I was being told wasn't in there. It was something different for each application. I had to again stare at the words "You're missing something" and laugh or cry. I looked at Joe and said, "I don't think I'm supposed to go to law school."

He said, "I was wondering how long it would take you to figure that out."

Don't get me wrong, I'm proud to be a medium, but

when you have your mind set on what you want, it's hard to see another picture.

I've heard stories from other people who were changing jobs and weren't sure which direction to go and asked for a sign. They received a call the same day from an associate starting a new business venture, wondering if they were interested. When my cat Sinbad was sick, I asked for a sign to know whether I should put him to sleep. I had a dream that night where my friend Domini thumbed through my scrapbooks, then she waved at me to follow her, and she walked me through a door. As I walked through, I found myself standing in my vet's office. Domini smiled at me, letting me know it would be all right. My mom took Sinbad to the vet the next day. I couldn't go because I knew he wouldn't be coming home with me, and it broke my heart. The vet looked at Sinbad and said that he had terminal cancer and that it was painful. So we did the humane thing and let him go. Not easy, but Domini's sign let me know that it was the right thing to do and that she'd take care of him. Signs come in many forms for many different reasons. They serve as both comfort and guidance when heeded. If you're lucky enough to be given a sign, pay attention. Sometimes the consequences of ignoring them are minor, but often we think back and we could kick ourselves for ignoring a sign sent to guide us.

May 8, 2005, was not only a beautiful Sunday afternoon but Mother's Day. Joe, my mom, myself, and our three girls were off to the mall for a shoe-shopping spree because my mom and I agreed nothing would be more fun. My plan was to pick up my grandma after our shopping trip and have her join us for dinner. While we were driving, I informed my mom that I wanted to get Grandma Jenee later for dinner.

My mom began joking and said, "Do we have to?" She had just taken Grandma to lunch earlier and was teasing, as most daughters will.

I turned to my mom to say, "Mom, this is Grandma's last Mother's Day, so be nice."

In between the words *Mother's* and *Day,* a huge pigeon hit my windshield. My face and the bird were separated only by a piece of glass. We were all completely floored. In my whole life I've never hit an animal in my car, ever. The bird came out of the sky and flew right into our windshield. It wasn't just the bird, it was the bird coupled with the words that were coming out of my mouth at the time. I was speaking of my grandmother's imminent death! I had just talked to my brother Michael about it the night before.

He had said, "Something's different with Grandma. Al, Grandma *feeeels* different. I know she's gonna go this year, but I can't put my finger on the feeling."

I said, "Michael, the feeling is that she's already gone."

"Yes!" he said. "That's it! That's what it feels like."

"Michael, whenever you get that feeling in the future, you'll know the person's days are numbered. That's how mediums learn to read things."

I snapped back to the ride to Grandma's house, thinking of what I'd miss the most about her. There are so many things. The fact that she loves hummingbirds and has had a feeder for them my whole life. Her great laugh and the way she lights up when Joe and I take the kids over to her house to visit.

This was indeed a special Mother's Day. I made an emotional note to savor the day. As I gazed at my grandma from across the dinner table, I remembered her taking me to the park to feed the ducks and how she'd braid my hair too tight when I was little. So tight I thought my eyes would reach my ears. Okay, that was a slight exaggeration, but you know what I mean. I handed Grandma her Mother's Day gift. She loves cash, so she squealed with delight as she reached for her purse. She pulled out a picture of a lavender dress, hat, and purse, along with an order form. She explained how badly she wanted this outfit but that it required she save money in order to buy it. I knew what this dress was; it was what she was going to be buried in. I knew it, my mom knew it, and even Joe knew it.

"Grandma, can I see that?"

She handed me the form, where she had already filled in all her information ready to send to buy this outfit that she adored. I flipped open my cell phone and dialed the number.

My grandma said, "Allison, what are you doing?"

I noticed my grandma had added the amount wrong, and I wanted to make sure that she had this outfit to enjoy when it mattered the most, *before* her final day of rest.

As we sat waiting for dinner, I ordered my grandma that outfit, and she couldn't have smiled any bigger. Everyone at our table was so moved to see Grandma so happy. Sometimes it's the little things in life that mean everything. I'm sharing this with you because I want you to see my life and walk through it with me. Maybe one day you will relate to my experiences. Maybe you already do.

In the spring of 2004 I made a prediction. I said that I would lose my grandmas within twelve months of each other. My grandmas are very different women, nothing alike. My grandma Lesa (stepgrandma, but I loved her) was Italian, fiery, and enormously loving. Grandma Maria (my dad's mom) was Hispanic, adored my dad, and loved to cook. The grandma I'm the closest to, my grandma Jenee (my mom's mom), is European, tall, friendly, loves to play the piano, and is a medium.

In October 2004 my grandma Lesa passed away to join my grandfather Joseph, whom I adore. In December 2004 my grandma Maria died to join her son, my dad, where I know she's the happiest. My grandma Jenee is not doing so well, and I'm trying to spend time with her and let her know how much she means to me. Although I am fortunate enough to still have my grandma Jenee with me, I know I won't have her forever. My grandma knows she is getting up there and jokes that she's so bad that hell doesn't even want her. This cracks me up, and I know it's not true. I tell her she's "still needed," that's all.

I always tell her she can't go anywhere, because "then

I'll be the bad one in the family," and we laugh. I was shaken by the bird's hitting the windshield, as was everyone in the car. I read it as a sign, and I understand that an end is most likely coming. For now, I'm just keeping my fingers crossed that last Mother's Day, when the bird incident happened, won't be the last one that I get to spend with my grandmother.

Somebody's Baby

This chapter is dedicated to all the children who miss their mom or dad. Whether you were eight weeks old or eighty years old when your parent died, we are all little kids inside when it comes to our mom and dad. Some parents I bring through in readings express regret for not spending more time with their kids. They share that they'd do things differently now and that they try to take care of you from the other side, make it up to you, if it's in their power. The problem with dying and leaving behind wounded people is that, once you've passed, often the wounded no longer want your help. That's why I tell people if you live well, you die well. In other words, when you paint the portrait of your life, be sure it's a picture you can look at forever, because you will. This doesn't mean we can't forgive people after their death. It's just nicer to have those moments while you can still hold them.

Maybe your dad was father of the year because he was always your rock during your emotional storms and your pillow when you needed a place to cry. Or he could have been one of those men who had to learn later on how to be a good dad. Maybe he wasn't good at "I love you." Or maybe he missed all those nights when you were small, failing to tuck you in. The same goes for moms. Maybe you were blessed enough to have a mom who could rival Carol Brady for the ultimate mom award. Maybe you weren't raised by your mom and didn't get to bond with her in life. Either way, I hope this chapter reminds you all that you are loved and adored by those who gave you life. Even those who had to see with their own eyes where they went wrong and how they can help you now.

As a medium, I am glad to lend my assistance to others, helping them to move through their pain after losing someone they love. After my dad died, I found myself needing solace from the other side and had to learn to accept the kindness of others. I was accustomed, being a medium, to my ability to make contact with the other side at my will. This is how I had planned on moving myself forward when my dad died, because it was the best way I knew to heal myself. Now I would be taught an unfamiliar lesson, how to accept the help I needed from someone who had no agenda other than to act as a mirror of myself, showing me what I do for others, putting me in the seat of the client.

Should I Take a Message?

When my dad passed away in September 2002, I found myself unable to see him or hear him for quite some time, which frustrated me greatly. I received a call a little less than a year after my dad died from a fellow research medium named Laurie Campbell. She apologized for not having called sooner, but she had just learned that my dad had died several months ago. She also shared that her own dad had passed recently. We spoke of the frustration of being mediums and being able to see the dead but not being able to see our own dads. This didn't sit well with us, not because of ego, but because we live in the trenches of life and death in our profession. Our work is a part of who we are, and so are our fathers, yet neither of us seemed to be able to communicate with our own father. As Laurie and I spoke on the phone, it occurred to us that we could see and hear each other's father. Could we read each other? Give closure to another medium?

Laurie confidently stated, "Allison, your dad says he prefers blondes."

She laughed hysterically and so did I.

I responded, "Laurie, you could have told me anything about my dad, and you said what was paramount to who my father was and is. My dad *loooved* blondes and always said so." She continued to talk about his being dressed in a tuxedo and how regal he looked. She continued to fill my head with details about my dad that were very personal. I was immersed in a comfort that I recognized as something that I was used to providing for others, and I then understood why my clients were so full of gratitude after a reading.

I told Laurie, "I see your dad too, and he's cracking nuts and eating them. He's also referring to your daughter Amanda as 'Peanut.' " This turned out to be a nickname he had called his granddaughter. Laurie's dad likes to share things with me such as what's in Laurie's kitchen pantry, or what object is sitting in front of Laurie while we talk on the phone. I told her that her dad kept talking about the man in the navy and the name Ronald connected to him. She confirmed for me that her uncle (her mom's brother) was in the navy and his name is Ron. I kept seeing a 1957 Chevy in my head that was connected to her family. She confirmed that it belonged to her parents and she still has pictures of it. Her dad kept talking about Santa Cruz as a place where a family member had lived, which I conveyed to Laurie. She said that her grandma used to live there and they drove there in the '57 Chevy when Laurie was two or three years old to visit. Her dad then showed me a Felix the Cat clock with the eyes shifting from side to side. Laurie said that her grandma from Santa Cruz had one in her house. I kept seeing salmon and eggs, and her dad said they used to make them a lot, which Laurie confirmed. Laurie's dad spoke fondly about the ham and scalloped potato casserole that they used to make. This was special to Laurie, having him acknowledge something that she used to make for him. He kept talking about a black skillet that Laurie's mom always cooked with when she'd make him fried eggs.

I kept seeing a patchwork cat that her dad kept showing me, and he said they had one. Laurie confirmed the patchwork cat that her mom had made in her house growing up. Her dad also talked about being around "Bill" on the other side, and Laurie shared that he was her dad's father. Her dad kept saying the name "Scooter" and talked about being around Scooter, and it turned out that was the name of Laurie's sister's cat that had died. I was shown horses and cowboy boots as connected to Laurie's dad. Laurie's sister ended up getting a new horse around that time that matched the description of the horse that her dad had shown me. Her dad also said that he had to go "in order to keep Laurie's kids here." I shared this with Laurie. Although it didn't make sense at the time, being a medium, she knew it would mean something someday. A couple of years after Laurie's dad's death, Laurie found out that her son needed a heart transplant. Laurie was naturally frantic and she said, "Allison, is he going to get a heart?" I told her he would.

Some months after that, her son was offered a heart that I had a bad feeling about. Laurie shared this feeling. Laurie called and asked, "Allison? Should I take the heart? If I pass on it, he may die before he's offered another one." It's an emotional and difficult question to answer for a client who's frantic. It was tearing me apart to hear my answer for my friend. "Laurie, reject the heart. It's a weak heart, and it will make him ill."

She did, she turned it down, and it was one of the most difficult choices that she's ever had to make. It was also one of the most difficult things that I've ever had to say. The next day Laurie learned that there was a question about the donor's using drugs, which would have compromised the heart. As relieved as we were, we still knew that Laurie's son needed a heart for transplant.

Some weeks after that, Laurie was getting worried because another donor heart hadn't come up for her son. It was May at the time, and Laurie asked me if I could tell about what time a donor heart would come for him. I was nervous about being off on my prediction; this after all was life or death for a friend's son. "The Fourth of July, Laurie, he'll get it on the Fourth of July." The Fourth of July weekend came, and we celebrated my youngest daughter's fifth birthday. There were little girls everywhere and red, white, and blue cake smeared across their pretty little faces. My phone rang. It was Laurie: "Allison, they have a heart that's a match. They're performing the transplant on the fourth, just like you said."

I gave her my love and prayers, and we hung up. Her son had the transplant and everything went smoothly. Her dad did keep him here and watched over him during the heart transplant and after. Laurie's dad and my dad shared too many details, names, places, and other information to name them all, but you get the gist of what I'm saying.

Laurie was moved by her dad's words and knew he was beside her, as I knew my dad was beside me from Laurie's information.

As time passed, we continued to read each other and laugh with our dads, something we thought we'd never do again. That was definitely a bonding experience, and since then we've had many conference phone calls for the four of us.

Another occasion that I had to put my pride aside and accept the supporting words of another was provided to me not by another medium but by a client.

I had a colleague call in a favor one Sunday afternoon when I was asked to give a reading for a friend of his. I normally don't work on Sunday, but I made an exception for him. My client showed up, a very vibrant woman with an air of wisdom about her. I invited her in and we sat down. I looked at her and said, "I get the issue is your dad." I then went into special details about her dad, who had passed away. At the end of her reading, I shared with her that my dad too had passed and I understood her pain. It's strange when you lose someone you love; sometimes the only comfort you really find is in those who have walked your same path. For me it was another daughter who'd lost the first man she'd ever loved too, her dad. You'd think that would be the end of the story, but not so. Later that day, after my client left, I received an e-mail from her. She wrote, "I know this is going to sound crazy, but after I left the reading, while I was driving home, I could hear what I believe was your dad, Allison. He was singing a song called "Last Dance" by, I think, Donna Summer. Does that make sense to you? I know I don't know you or your dad, but I thought I'd tell you anyway."

I sat back in my office chair and stared at the words on my computer screen as though I were consuming the words with my eyes. Does that make sense to me? I thought. Well, let me tell you how much that means to me. After Dad died, every time I walked into a building, that song would come on. I knew it was my dad saying we had our "last dance." When I had to change the title on his car and remove his name and add mine, it was a particularly difficult day. I stopped at a little tavern to process my pain, and like clockwork, "Last Dance" was the first song that came on when I sat down. Of course, I bawled like a baby, but still I knew the song was sent with love. Sometimes the things that remind us of those we love cause us pain, because the connection from the other side reminds us that our loved one isn't here on earth with us. But later those are the moments we will crave. I don't remember the exact moment, but after two years of hearing that song and choking back tears, I found that one day the pain became a smile. For an instant I caught myself smiling and I felt a little guilty, but I know my dad would rather I smile when I think of him than cry. I have given that time a great deal of thought, and I think that once I cracked my first smile and I fully owned that my dad was with me by not mourning him but embracing him, his energy, and love, the curtain between us fell. Now I say, "Hey, Dad, it's our song!" and I know he hears me.

My dad was a professional ballroom dancer for fifty years. We had our last dance together in September 1999 at my cousin Juan's sixtieth birthday party. My family certainly knows how to throw a memorable party. I was seated with my husband, Joe, and my dad at a round table that afforded me the luxury to be able to take in everyone at the table at once. It was a calm night, and light hearts engulfed the moments that would connect like dots, ending in the last dance that I shared with my dad. My dad stood before me. "Come on, Allison, let's dance! Dance with your old dad."

"Oh Dad! I'm not good at the West Coast swing."

"Sure you are, you're my daughter."

"Oh yeah, what was I thinking?"

We laughed and we danced, my dad with an enormous smile on his face that left anyone helpless but to notice him. His infectious smile had a domino effect throughout the celebration, reminding all that my dad was never anything less than the life of the party. My dad danced with me from the time that I was an infant until, like any good party, his life came to an end. Anyone who has loved another will understand how important a song can be and the power that a song has to resurrect memories and share good times as though they were happening in real time.

And remember that, even though you may not be a "medium," that doesn't mean there won't ever be a day that you will have a medium-like experience. Some people have fleeting medium-like experiences, some people only once in a lifetime. I see it like any ability; some people have more of a certain talent than others. When you're ten years old, you can have the baseball game of a lifetime, a game that is still legendary in your family or your town, to be recounted for generations to relive. You won the big game against the town rival, and you were a hero for it. You grow up and never have that experience again, but you know it's possible, and you recognize the feeling. Another ten-year-old child goes on to play pro ball and eventually enters the Hall of Fame. A town hero and a Hall of Famer can both experience their moment of greatness and revel in it.

It is these moments that bring us fulfillment in life. Sometimes a moment of greatness comes in the form of a homemade birthday card that your little one made for you. This is no regular card but a one-of-a-kind card that displays your child's love for you, which can be seen on her little cherry-drink-stained smile as she hands you the card that she meticulously crafted with pride. People walk different paths and often wonder why they can't do something that you can and vice versa. It's because, sometimes, a taste of an experience is all that you needed to know that you're a part of something bigger than you are and to be reminded how much you've loved being a part of it.

If you're given a message from the other side, don't be afraid to share it. My client shared my father with me by confirming his sign to me through the title of the song. Even though she wasn't a professional medium, her words meant everything to me because I knew she had delivered a message from him. You never know how much the most seemingly obscure detail will mean to the recipient. Be sensitive to the message and circumstances. If it's a downer of a message that won't help anybody, then write the message down and throw it away. Energetically tossing it out rids you of the negativity. It's kind of like making a big statement that you aren't going to internalize the information. Most of us are aware that bad news can manifest physically within us if we carry too much baggage. This is a good exercise for anyone who needs to get distance from a bad situation. Usually, big problems come with a first name, and writing the name down and throwing it away lets you affirm your decision to move on. Works for me!

If it's upbeat information, then share it. Be sure the recipient is open to life after death. If you don't know the person well enough to know this about him or her, then a warm smile is more appropriate than a message from those passed. Either way, appreciate the gift of the message and the knowledge that we're not alone.

I had another experience after my dad died that brought me a lot of comfort and acted as a shining example of how mediums can also be blocked by pain and have to receive messages from their clients or another source. Occasionally the sign will benefit more than either a client or the medium; it may help all involved.

I was meeting with a wonderful woman in November of 2004 for a reading. She was a client, and hers had been the last private reading that I would be able to do that year because of the time demands of the holidays, family, *Medium*'s debut, press, and so on. Joe had thought about rearranging the date of the reading, but I told him, "I'm supposed to read her. It's important, so messing with the schedule could be bad."

When she arrived, we sat down and exchanged pleasantries. Her mom came through and shared many personal details with me that I passed along to her. So as we sat and laughed at her mom's effervescent sense of humor, my client said to me, "Allison, that's all great and it means a lot, really, but could she tell you the nickname she had for me?"

I said, "I can ask, but I can only give you what she gives me."

So I asked her mom for the nickname, and I concentrated and listened with everything I had, and I heard nothing. The silence was deafening; the moments were long and empty. In actuality, it was only a minute, but it felt like forever. I apologized to her because I could see how disappointed she was.

Just then I heard my dad, whom I had only recently

started to hear two years after his passing. He said, "Allison, tell her about the nickname I have for you."

So I looked at her, and I said, "For some reason my dad wants me to share my nickname with you that he called me for thirty years until his death. It's a little embarrassing though."

She smiled politely and said, "What is it?"

"Jellybean. He called me Jellybean because I was so physically tiny when I was little. Even when I grew bigger, he still called me Jellybean."

I saw her face fall, and I wondered if I had said something to offend her.

"Oh my God! Allison, that's the nickname my mom called me!"

Well, you could have knocked both of us over with a feather. Jellybean is not a common nickname. We were both stunned. We stared at each other for a few minutes with smiles on our faces and tears in our eyes. This happened at the end of her reading, and it put her over the top. I will never, as long as I live, forget that night. Neither one of us ever thought we'd be called that name again, and clearly our parents worked in concert to touch us both and remind us how loved we are by them and they by us. My client walked away with the satisfaction of knowing that she had visited with her mom that night and that her mom had had a lot to say. My client also had a lot to share with her living family, letting them know that she had been reassured first-hand that her mom would always be close by.

In September 2005, while finishing this book, I was summoned out of town by the fifty-seventh annual Emmy Awards. Patricia Arquette was nominated for Best Actress in a Drama for the show *Medium.* This was a moment in my life I will never forget, not just because of the honor involved, but because my dad paid me a visit.

I'm always telling people to watch the chairs at their family gatherings, because during the holidays our deceased relatives and friends want to be there too. They love to be there for special occasions. They will show up around whoever made them the happiest in life. Sometimes they show up to a house where they were the most content, and especially they'll appear if they get both of these things in one place. Most of the time, their visits have more to do with the people than the structure, though. I find it amusing to watch a common spirit interaction with the living. There will be a chair that nobody will sit in; the living will even walk around the chair and stare as though there's something in front of them that can't be seen but is felt. People will even prefer standing before sitting in the only chair in the room that's empty, and they don't really know why that is. Well, it's because the seat is already taken by a well-intending spirit who wants in on the occasion, so save them a seat!

This very occurrence happened to me at the Emmys. So, I'm at the Emmys, and Joe and I take our seats, drinking in the moment. Me and the mister are sitting at the Emmys for a show that was inspired by my life story, and the woman who plays me (Patricia Arquette) is up for an Emmy for Best Actress. Yeah, that was hard to wrap my mind around. So, the place is full of people all dressed up, and I have a knot in my stomach that keeps reminding me how nervous I am. I wanted Patricia to win, she deserved to win, and she plays me, so I felt a vested interest.

Joe was sitting to my right at the end of the row. The seat next to me was empty; even the seat fillers who are on standby wouldn't sit there. This was a three-hour event, and my publicist's boss sat there for twenty minutes halfway through the night, and then it was vacant again. I looked at Joe and said, "Isn't it funny that nobody will sit there. Every chair is filled but that one."

Even the publicist who sat there briefly seemed uncomfortable, leaned over to me, and said, "I'm gonna go to the lobby. I'll see you later."

The moment of truth came before they were going to announce the winner of Best Actress in a Drama. The knot in my stomach grew, and I said, "Dad, I know you've been beside me tonight, and this is in no way a challenge. If Patricia wins, I will know that you, Patricia's dad, and Granddad had something to do with tonight, and I'll never question that you were here beside me."

The next words that I heard were "The winner is Patricia Arquette for *Medium*!"

I cried and looked down at my father's ring, which looked so out of place on my hand, and I rubbed it.

"Thanks, Dad, not for the win, but for being here with me on this special night. It means so much to me to have you here."

I kissed Joe and took all of the hugs headed my way, and we were off to the parties. When I walked into the Paramount/*Entertainment Tonight* party, I saw Patricia standing at a table that was clearly composed of people connected to *Medium*. I walked over, and she whirled around, handed me the Emmy, gave me a great hug, and said, "Thank you."

I was out of pithy responses, so I replied, "You're welcome."

A moment in time, that's what that was. She looked beautiful, and she was having the time of her life on a night that celebrated her talent. We posed for pictures and had a glass of champagne to toast the occasion, and as my glass and Joe's touched, the song "Last Dance" came on. Joe shot me a knowing look, and I was forced to lip-sync the rest of the song. Okay, not forced, but how could I resist? As of September 22, 2005, three years since Dad died, that song has gone from being a heartbreaker for me to a moment of celebration on a night that is a once-in-a-lifetime experience. Although I will always miss the way it was when my dad was living, I still have the comfort of knowing that when it's important to me, whether it be good times or bad times, he'll be there. It was icing on the cake that Patricia is a blonde and my dad had a clear affinity for blondes. Don't think that little detail escaped me.

———————

There are many ways that our loved ones, especially parents, take care of us still, even after their demise. I've seen
it for my clients, and I've seen it for myself. In September
2004, I got a really bad feeling that I was going to have a car
accident. So I slowed down, took alternate routes, and
guess what, I still got into a car accident.

Sometimes we're warned, but that doesn't mean we get
to avoid it. The warning just helps to prepare us for a shaky
situation.

So anyway, I was hit by a pickup truck, and I was really
mad. I loved my car. So I called Joe to come get me from the
scene of the accident. Of course, he wanted to take me to
the hospital, but I'm thickheaded like everyone else in my
family.

So I said, "Joe, I have a concussion, but I'm fine. Just
wake me up from time to time for a day or two."

Joe was pretty annoyed with me but is well aware he
can't change my mind.

I went out to my back porch and sat down to collect myself, which was not easy. I looked up at the sky and said,
"Wow, I was hit in the head pretty hard. Maybe I won't be
able to see or hear the dead anymore."

As I nervously laughed, I heard my father clearly say,
"You can hear me."

I almost fell off my chair. I knew my dad was with me

when I was in my accident because I could feel him, but that was the first time in two years that I was able to really hear him. When I left the scene of the accident, the first song that came on the radio was "Circle of Life" by Elton John, and I knew Dad was letting me know he was with me, which reinforced what I had already felt. My dad used to play "name that tune" with me. I was quite good, as he expected from me. So my dad communicates with me a lot through music when I'm experiencing something traumatic.

Dad's music would become especially important to me on August 30, 2005. I had spent a couple of days with Craig from *TV Guide* and Jennifer, my publicist from Paramount. Craig was writing a story on a day in the life of the real Allison DuBois. My life is never boring, so the first day they accompanied me to a radio interview with Tim and Willy from KNIX radio. These are two of my favorite radio personalities, and they happen to be in Phoenix. Later that night Craig, Jennifer, Joe, and I had dinner with a couple of the district attorneys whom I work with. We went to one of my favorite restaurants, Durant's in Phoenix; they have the best steaks and strawberry shortcake ever!

When I woke up the next day, I told Joe I was feeling "off" and irritated. Later that day I went to a farewell lunch with Craig and Jennifer. My cell phone rang and it was Joe: *"The girls are okay. Allison, I was in an accident. You need to come to the scene."*

Craig ran out the door with me, and we jumped into my

car. The radio came on when I started the engine. The song that was on was "Circle of Life."

I knew my dad was letting me know that he was with Joe and the girls and that everything would be okay. It didn't fall short on me that the same song had played one year ago, almost to the day, after my accident. I arrived at the scene. My two younger girls ran to me and held on tight. My eyes met Joe's. I saw his arm that had lost many layers of skin. I've brought through many spouses who have died in car accidents. Now my clients' feeling of loss all came rushing back to me. I counted myself immediately lucky and thanked God that my family was all right. The old lady who had hit my husband's car was being wheeled by on a paramedic's gurney. She apparently didn't see Joe and took a left into his car. While she was being wheeled by, my middle daughter looked at Craig and said, "It's okay, she doesn't have long to live anyway."

Obviously Craig and Jennifer were shocked. My youngest daughter then looked at Craig and said, "She has a TV in her head. She sees these things."

My other daughter angrily scolded her baby sister for telling anyone about that. Jennifer looked at my concerned daughter and said, "It's okay, your mom has a TV in her head too."

This is one of the ways little predictors and mediums express themselves and is good to note for parents who think that their kids might be gifted. I talked to my daughter later: "Honey, you can't say things like that about people you see dying. It's a big deal, and you need to be sensitive."

At the accident, my daughter said she was sorry, and with a crimson face, I apologized to Craig and Jennifer, who were incredibly supportive and understanding.

Joe looked at me and said, "You not only told me in the last three weeks that you saw me getting into a car accident, which made me be more cautious, but you told me a year ago when I bought the car that you saw me getting into an accident and to be careful."

I knew he was going to be in an accident, which clearly I couldn't stop. I saw the driver's side front fender being hit. It's very hard to "see" something that will hurt someone you love, but by being with Joe, I knew my dad was saying, "You couldn't save me, but I could save him." Without a doubt, with a wink of his eye. Thanks, Dad!

This is one of the ways they show us they love us from the other side, by intervening when they're permitted to. By the way, I wasn't the only one to see the accident before it happened. My eight-year-old daughter saw the accident in her head that day at lunch, right before it happened, and told her dad to "drive carefully."

As a footnote, just so you know, I did have a concussion and I am just fine. Joe's fine too. I told him to leave the crash dummy testing to me and never to scare me like that again. We laughed and hugged. Know this, that those we love and lost continue to protect us and when necessary give us a good swift kick in the posterior. Sometimes that's just what we need.

The loss of a parent is always tragic, but even more so when the children didn't have the opportunity to get to know their mom or dad or to make memories that they can find comfort in after their parent has passed. For these children, mediums can sometimes provide the first and most special details of a relationship that a parent has built from the other side.

EILEEN

The day was January 29, 1970; my father lay dead on the floor, a single gunshot wound to his head. I was a baby resting in my cradle, only a few feet away from a father I'd never know. At just under four months old, I wasn't a very good witness.

"Suicide," the cops declared. The same cops who for years would arrest my father for any petty crime that took place in our town. The same police force his brother served. No investigation, no fuss. Never mind that the gun he was holding in one hand didn't match the side of his head with the entrance wound. All agreed, suicide.

Our family knew another story. It seems that at some point he had made an enemy of an acquaintance who was part of organized crime. One night, badly beaten and left for dead outside, my dad, his friends, and our family were threatened. He was told that if he showed his face in a certain part of town again, he would not live to see his next birthday.

It seems my father did not heed the warning. His birthday was January 30 but he would not live to blow out birthday candles this year. He had been so proud to be a father, and he was really trying to turn his life around. He was doing public service speaking engagements to children in local schools, on the radio, and on TV.

Anyone who knew Chris said he would not have taken his own life. To this day his policeman brother says he never believed his death to be suicide. Friends have teased that his vanity was so great, he certainly wouldn't have ever shot himself in the head.

Fast-forward to October 2, 2004. I met Allison for the first time. Having lived with this pain in my heart throughout my life, I longed to find some peace. I'd hoped she would confirm what I've always believed to be true. During my reading my father "came through," and he apologized to me for my having to live with the shame involved with his death. He wanted me to know that someone else "had a hand" in his death. He said he knew it was coming and wanted to stop it, but he couldn't. He wanted to say he was sorry for not being there for my mother, and he acknowledged that she has not been there for me. He thanked my husband for loving me and being there for me to share my life "the way he would have been." He wanted to thank me for naming my children after him. No one, he said, had ever done anything so special for him in his life.

"Did you?" Allison asked after the reading.

Indeed. All five of our daughters' middle names are after my dad.

My fifth child was born twenty-nine years after he died on January 29, the anniversary of my dad's death, when I was twenty-nine years old. She was born spontaneously (in the bathtub) within the same half hour listed on his death certificate.

At my reading with Allison, my father then wished me a happy birthday. The lights in the room flickered. We all looked up, and Allison asked, "Is it your birthday?" As I answered in the affirmative, the lights flickered again. We all laughed.

The person responsible for taking my father's life will never be held accountable. But to receive validation from Allison has helped fill a void with some peace. I've always known the truth in my heart, but to hear it from Allison, after having only just met her that day, was overwhelming. The fact that she could tell me details unique between my father and me was incredibly special. She has given me such an amazing gift. She's provided me with a playback of the last moments of my dad's life, ending the not-knowing that had eaten at me for years. She also spoke all the words that I have waited my whole life to hear. I'll always be grateful to her for that.

My Take on Eileen's Reading

I ask my client to not give me information before a reading on the person who passed away, their relationship to my client, or the cause of passing. A medium should be able to give the client the information. Clients can feel free to confirm and ask questions after the initial information has already been provided, but it's necessary for the medium to give information first. It makes a reading more compelling.

Eileen had seen me on a news program in Phoenix, where I was tested on the air when I was asked to read a person that the news station had selected. After watching me, she decided that she wanted to book a reading. Her reading was scheduled for October 2, 2003, which coincidentally is my wedding anniversary. Before a client comes, I always write a few pages of information that is given to me by the deceased connected to my client. When I met Eileen and her husband, Paul, I had the information that I had previously written down on her dad and his passing on a pad of paper resting in my lap. Eileen walked into my office—a statuesque, dark-haired woman, not only a classic beauty on the outside, but every bit as pretty within. Paul, her husband, reminded me of my Joe. He's supportive of Eileen, and it is easy to see the deep love he has for his wife. I told Eileen that I was picking up on a father figure who had passed away. He was very insistent that I tell her that he did not take his own life and that he'd never have willingly left her.

He also kept showing a money transaction as being involved in his murder. He knew the killer and let him into his house willingly, not expecting that it would be the last person he would see before he died. Chris showed me this event in slow motion because not a lot of time passed and he wanted me to feel the enormity of those few last moments of his life. When Chris showed me the scene, it was slightly out of focus, so I had to look hard to understand why. Sometimes when a person has had a drink of alcohol at the time of death, it can impair what I see too. This is only the case when they show me the scene through their eyes.

Chris talked me through the details surrounding his death, which I shared with Eileen. Some of the details I'm leaving out because they're personal to Eileen and not appropriate to share. Of all the details that Chris shared, I find the most important information to be the way he died. He did not commit suicide; he was murdered by a hired hit man. He said that he loves his little girl and would never have left her for any reason. That he was at Eileen's wedding in spirit and thought she looked beautiful. That he's honored to have five granddaughters named after him. He spends a lot of time around the girls, all of his lovely granddaughters, but most important and especially his little girl.

When spirits show me a meaningful moment that they are a part of, sometimes it's through their eyes. Sometimes it's just an overview of the room where a pivotal action took place. When greed is involved, and a money transaction is a part of why they died, they often show me a black bag full of money so that I understand the motive for their murder. Spirits find many ways to communicate, but their main goal with a medium is to get us to understand what they're saying and to help us to deliver their message to those they love.

Losing a parent is like losing a part of yourself. Every day after is a journey forward that teaches us perseverance. Our love for those we lost provides us incentive to strengthen our memory so as to not forget all the little details of their faces, their laughs, anything that brings them back to us, if only for a moment. Children find different ways to heal or at least to move forward. We who have lost parents will find them again in the faces of our children or in a dream where they make a special appearance. For the daughters and sons who still have their parents in the living world, enjoy every Mother's Day, Father's Day, every moment when they remind you of when you were small, because right now you are creating the very moments that you will replay in your mind over and over later.

I still miss my dad. I think that never really goes away. Sometimes I watch *Father of the Bride* with Steve Martin and bawl like a baby, but you know what? I couldn't possibly cry like that if my dad hadn't done something right in life. I know I'm not the only daughter who cries when she watches movies like that, thinking of the dad she lost. I know how hard it is, especially for the kids who lost their parents young, and my heart goes out to them. I think I speak for everyone on that note. My dad used to call me "Jellybean." As I grew older, I hated it, but now I love that he saw me as little and sweet. It's funny how your perspective changes, isn't it?

CHAPTER 6

Angels of the Hospice

While writing this book, I have ventured where most people can't bear to go, into a hospice, where I watched a friend let go. My friend's name was Shari.

Shari wasn't my biological parent, although she was like a mom to me for all of my life. I met Shari when I was an infant. My closest childhood friend, Susie, is her daughter. Shari was my mom's best friend, and boy, did they have fun together. I can't remember a time in the beginning of my life when she wasn't there. Shari and my mom took Susie and me to Knott's Berry Farm when I was ten, and we had so much fun that our heads hurt from laughing so much. We drove from Arizona to California in a big, pale yellow station wagon with my boom box thumping. I'm sure that my mom drove as fast as that wagon would take us so that she could get away from the same two songs that I played all the way there. I believe one of the songs was "Girls Just Want to Have Fun" by Cyndi Lauper, and wasn't it the truth? We were making a memory so special that when I grew up, it would be a part of the soul that makes up this book.

Yeah, it seemed like it was Shari and my mom against the world. Sitting by our swimming pool, laughing together, is how I remember Shari and my mom. We never quite knew what they had in those big, bright plastic tumblers that they drank out of when Susie and I were small. Susie and I laugh about it now, because we can wager a guess on what beverage would make our moms increasingly giggly as they drank another round. Susie and I were splashing around in the water with a beautiful big sun watching over us. The promise of Happy Meals from our moms guaranteed a big "Yeah!" from our little mouths.

Yep, our moms were the coolest. Shari was larger than life with her red hair and her hippie bandana wrapped around her head, tied at the nape of her neck. My mom, the stunning blonde, turned heads with her floppy, big-brimmed hat and her Hollywood good looks. They were young and setting the world on fire together.

Now I had to realize that, as much as I'd like to turn back the clock to give Shari a day of being healthy again, it was not in my power. Many others out there understand what I'm saying because they too have their memories and their own clock that they'd like to turn back.

I had just found out that Shari was going to die. She had pancreatic, lung, and liver cancer. There was no hope for survival. I ventured into the hospice where she had been moved after a stay in the hospital. Visiting a hospice is like no other experience. Hospices are full of people who are sick and terrified and who know that they'll never go home again.

I stared down at the woman who tried to feed me carrots when I was two. She always laughed, telling the story of the stubborn two-year-old who tried to explain to her that I was "leeergic to carrots." I wasn't and she knew it; I just didn't want to eat them. So she made me something else to pacify me. I'm sure it involved a high sugar content, because Shari was always baking pastries of some sort. Shari was not only a vibrant, loving, funny woman, she was a nurse who cared for the sick and dying herself. She worked until the day she entered the hospital, never to walk out again.

I learned something sitting beside Shari. I learned that the dying force us to feel things that we would never voluntarily feel. They make us face our own mortality and force us to ask why. They force us to put ourselves in their shoes, and then force us to tell them all the things that we love about them, words that we shouldn't have waited so long to say. Some people never say the words at all, which is a shame. They fight to hold on to life out of the habit of living.

They need to hear you say that it's okay to let go. Otherwise they just keep on fighting. A voice they trust, telling them to let go, telling them you love them and always will love them, is an enormous comfort to those who are dying.

I watched my mom hold her dying friend's hand firmly, yet with loving care. I watched my mom carefully apply Shari's favorite color of bright pink lipstick to Shari's lips. She called Shari "princess" and gave her a manicure. She was learning how to love Shari in a way that made it comfortable for Shari to let go and allowed my mom to let go of the way things had been in the past.

I sat beside Shari's bed and replayed every memory that I had stored of my mom and Shari getting into mischief together in the 1970s and 1980s, when they were learning how to be single moms together. We lived in the same cul de sac, and when one would be down and out, the other one was there, either with money to make ends meet or a shoulder to cry on. I stared at Shari, the woman who had decided long ago that the best medicine for a skinned knee was for her to bake you a chocolate cake. She wasn't so wrong.

I sat next to Shari and I read her funny jokes and anecdotes by nurses, and Mom and I laughed. I stared at a poster board on the wall that said, "My name is Shari. I like rock music, funny movies, and pizza. I have two daughters and five granddaughters." I read it out loud to Shari, announcing who she is and letting her know that she's not just a person who happens to be dying. She's our friend, and she matters to many. We were there simply to love her and for no other reason. When people are dying, it's crucial that they have people with them who can reminisce with them and hold their hand. Shari was a natural comedian, so my telling nurse jokes was my way of connecting with that part of her. My mom has always been very aware of appearance and personal care. She showed Shari love by pampering Shari. My mom expanded the energy that Shari didn't have as a deep way of showing love.

The last moments of a person's life are as pivotal for the living as for the dying. Death allows us to perform those last acts of love for the person who's passing on. Shari kept saying "hot," she was burning up, and we couldn't do much to comfort her. Her organs were shutting down, and her body was not cooling itself well. We fed her ice chips and applied cool cloths to her forehead. It was all that we could do. I prayed that if Shari was not to be saved, God would please take her home so that she didn't have to suffer anymore. It physically pained me to hug her because I could feel her cancer, yet I didn't know how to let go. I asked my dad to help Shari over. I gazed at Shari one last time, knowing that I would never see her alive again. At the same time—and I'm sure many people can relate to this—as I looked at Shari, I knew that "my" Shari was already gone. The woman who was always laughing and pulling practical jokes on us, the woman who made us raspberry tarts for Christmas, the woman I grew up around had no more happy memories to create for herself or the ones who love her.

Just before we left, a friend of Shari's, who is also a nurse, walked in to see her. He shared that he hadn't seen Shari in a while before she was wheeled into the hospice. He gazed down at his dying friend with love, compassion, and, of course, heartbreak. It was profound to view the relationship between two people who, as nurses, had always cared for strangers as though they were family. Shari was now the patient, and it was something to see her friend, in the ultimate act of friendship, take care of the nurse whom he just happened to also love.

Even besides the hardship of facing the death of a friend, I find a hospice a particularly difficult place to be. I was bumping into those who had died as I walked down the hall. I felt numb, except for the prickly feeling on the surface of my skin that I always get when I'm around death or spirits. In this case, it was both. I felt like my senses were overloading. The dead would steal my breath every couple of minutes when they would try to move through me or talk to me. I glanced out of the window at the sunshine and the Christmas decorations that lined the houses in the area. All of a sudden, I felt like I was standing in a nucleus of death and beyond the walls resided the living. Part of me longed to rejoin the living, but right now I was needed by the dying. I wanted to walk into each room and hold the dying who had no visitors and let them know they're not invisible and remind them that they're still here. To tell all of them that they matter and, even when it seems they're alone, they're not.

I think a lot of people who are dying have the line

blurred between "here" and "there." They lose track of where life ends and eternal life begins. Most hospice nurses will tell you that the dying start talking about being little kids or telling detailed stories about their parents, who have been deceased for decades. The dying do this because they're sensing their youth again; they're feeling those who are waiting for them and are there to receive them. I've spoken with hundreds of people who've been in the room of the dying and witnessed the dying talking about being small or younger, or the dying saying they saw the deceased in their room in the last days of their life. I've also brought people through who talk about seeing the people who'd previously died right before they themselves passed and now say that they're together. The spirits give me names and physical descriptions of the visitors they had when they were alive.

I was deeply impressed with the hospice that Shari stayed in. It was warm, personal, and soothing. It was in a large house called the Gardener Home in Phoenix, donated to the hospice by the family that had lived there. It was being run by Hospice of the Valley. Such a good idea. I had never thought of what a gift donating a house to the dying would be. As I was thinking about this great gift, my mom said to me, "Should we have a chaplain come see Shari?"

I thought it a grand idea, one of the few comforts that we could provide for Shari. Although Shari didn't belong to a specific religion, she definitely believed in God. My mom and I told Shari we had to go but that we loved her. Shari whispered, "I love you too."

As we walked out of her room, a handsome older man with piercing blue eyes walked out of another patient's room and approached us.

"Can I help you? I'm a chaplain. Would you like for me to pray with your friend?"

This was no coincidence. He looked like an angel, he sounded like an angel, and that day he was our angel.

We joined hands with each other and Shari as he prayed for her and with her and, for the first time, I saw a look of peace cross Shari's face. That day there were many angels in that hospice. The nurses who are in the death trenches every day are angels; those dying, preparing to get "their wings," are angels; those who have already died and await their loved ones, those who died in the same hospice who stay to help others cross, the people who value the last wishes and moments of those who held them when they were children or sit beside those who were the children they held, they're all angels. Sometimes just someone whom you allowed to hold your hand is an angel.

As I said good-bye to a friend I love, it pained me because all I really wanted to do was pull Shari back, to give her my strength, and take some of her pain away. I know that this is unreasonable, but who wants to be reasonable when it comes to losing a friend? If love were enough, I suppose nobody would ever die. To the people who sit in hospices and say good-bye to the way things were, know that you're not alone. To those who work there, know that we appreciate you. To those who will die there, know that angels are tending to you and that you will not be forgotten.

The morning after I visited the hospice, I was emotionally wrung out, so I called my friend Kelly. I told her I wanted to call the hospice but was told by an inner voice, "Don't call right now."

As I sat on the phone talking to Kelly about Shari, just then I saw Shari in front of me. She always had an overstated sense of humor that I loved. Shari appeared before me in her peach-colored fairy godmother Halloween costume that she wore a couple of years back. Wings and wand included! The picture of her in this costume was hung on the wall of her hospice room. As I admired her healthy appearance and her always great humor, I had to crack a smile.

She said, "I'm gone."

"Kelly, Shari just showed herself to me and she said she's gone."

"Oh, Allison, I'm sorry." (It's nice having friends who don't question you because they already know your capabilities.)

Fifteen minutes later my other line rang. "Kelly, it's Hospice of the Valley. Hold on."

It was the news that I needed to hear from someone else. "Allison, Shari just passed away a little bit ago."

Me and my big mouth responded softly with "I know."

The family friend who was relaying this bad news to me

was okay with what I had said, but I have to be careful, it's not always easy to explain to others exactly where I'm coming from. I clicked back to my other line and shared the news with Kelly. It's not easy to get the words out with a lump in your throat. Just then a song came on by Bread (for those of you old enough to know who they are). It's called "Everything I Own." As I drank in the words, I knew it was from Shari. People who die like to reach the living through songs on the radio. Spirits seem to have an electric energy that can manipulate electronic items. What are radios? Boxes full of words about emotion, so it makes sense that spirits try to speak to us through the songs. They send their love that way, and many people know when a song has been sent to them by a loved one who passed away. They are and should be sure of it.

Shari had passed away. The only comfort for me is that I know when people die, they're strong, vibrant, happy, and beautiful. I see them in their new form after they pass; it's an immediate transformation. I know this because I saw Shari minutes after she passed and she looked radiant. Amazing, I saw Shari moments after she passed away, what a gift! She was glorious and smiling again. Till we meet again, Shari! I love you.

A few days after Shari died, I attended her funeral along with other friends and family. I took my seat waiting for the sermon. When I looked up, the same man with the piercing blue eyes who had prayed with us in the hospice was standing at the podium. He spoke lovingly and with conviction about Shari's life, a woman he had sat with in the last days of her life in the Hospice of the Valley, the woman whose hand he held and whose forehead he had placed his hand on as Shari struggled with dying. When he finished, I asked Shari's daughter, Susie, how they had arranged for him to give her mother's sermon. Susie was unaware of the connection between the blue-eyed man and her mother. She said that a friend of her mother's was across town at the hospital and met this really nice man who turned out to be a minister. He asked the man to speak at his friend's funeral, and the man accepted.

"Wow!" was all I could muster to say.

The minister was at a hospital at least forty minutes away from the hospice where he had met Shari when he was asked to speak at her funeral. He didn't realize that he was speaking at a funeral for a dying woman he had met across town days earlier. He spoke of his surprise when he laid eyes on Shari's picture placed on the table beside the podium at her funeral and realized that this was the same woman whom he had prayed for. Phoenix has millions of people in it. I know that it was no coincidence that this "angel" of a man, who gave Shari peace at the end of her life, also gave her peace in death. I cannot convey the look of shock on my face and my mother's when we laid eyes on him at Shari's funeral, but maybe you can imagine the calm he provided us in our hearts when we knew he was sent to us. We are sent whom and what we need when we need them the most.

The word P-A-I-N can never sum up what it feels like to lose someone. There is no word in any language that can fully describe the loss of one's self when someone dies. After writing this chapter, I realized something. Every moment that you take a step forward by making it through another day, no matter how good or bad you feel, you can't run fast enough or far enough to escape loss. This is because you can never leave behind the love inside your heart. It moves with you. It moves with you because the person who died stands beside you.

It's ironic. I see people who are living who walk through life feeling dead inside, just passing time until they die. Then there are those who have died who want to stay with the living and have never felt more alive. There are people who had a chemical imbalance in life who, now dead, want to join the living because they see how beautiful life can be. There are also souls who just had such a great life that they still want to share it with their loved ones. And there are people who died too soon who choose to remain with the living who are the same age so they can live through their experiences. There are people who fought to live an extra day, or to see one last sunset, and they fight for these things out of a love of life. Life is meant to inspire us to take a chance, to reach down into the very core of who we are and bring that to the surface to share.

I guess the trick is to "think outside the body" while you are living. How have you touched people and made their life better? Do you remember to send a birthday or Christmas card to relatives who have become distant and who might be alone? Do you plan a special night for you and your spouse to let your love know you appreciate him or her? I know widows/widowers who would give anything to have another day with the love of their life. Do you take the time to compliment people in passing to brighten their day? I do! I love making people smile, because it seems so much of my life involves people crying because they miss the ones they love. I love asking my grandma Jenee about her parents and when she was little. It makes her so happy to talk about them. I love bringing grandma her favorite foods and calling her for no other reason than to brighten her day. Grandma still has a lot to teach us in her older years, and she still needs company and acknowledgment, she's human! So I won't waste any time that I still have with my grandma, no regrets!

In my life, I know my oldest daughter will always remember me springing her from school to go shopping. It's not the shopping that mattered, it was that her mom was creating a moment with her. We ate junk food and laughed. I revel in my children. I ride roller coasters with them, hold them when they feel the world is against them. I will always fight for their happiness. I teach them to touch others. We take them to the mall every Christmas, and we buy a whole tree of Salvation Army Christmas Angels for kids without Christmas. My girls pick out everything personally. They will grow up to take the time to care about others, as Shari did in her life.

Caretakers

After going through the pain of losing Shari, I remembered fondly the hospice nurses. Nurses and people who work in hospices experience loss on a daily basis. They're often with the dying when no family or friends are there. I wanted to share with you a wonderful woman named Joani Roberts. She is a caretaker, and she serves as a surrogate family member for the dying and the family of the dying. I came to know her because my friend Brian's grandfather was ill in 2005. She took care of him during this time, and she was able to make his final moments of life better. She also brought Brian a great deal of comfort in knowing that his granddad was not just being taken care of but was being cared for like family.

Joani has many memories of sharing someone's final moments. I've asked her to relate one of them to you to show that almost anyone who chooses a career that deals with death will be faced with life after death.

SUZETTE

Suzette was an eighty-year-old, white female who came into hospice service with colon cancer. She had been married to Phil for fifty-five years. One night, sixteen hours before her passing, I was sitting quietly at her bedside, in the dark, when she asked me to please turn the TV off. I gently took her hand and told her that the TV wasn't on. She spoke of a movie screen playing above her bed. She asked, "You don't see it? You don't see the nuns? I'm sitting there in my uniform, it's me."

I said, "No, but tell me about it."

She said, "It's my life, and it's loud. Will you turn it off?"

I said, "I sure will."

I sat quietly for a few moments, and inquired, "Is that better?"

She said, "Yes."

I thought she had drifted peacefully to sleep. Fifteen minutes later, in the darkness, she asked, "Have you met my father?"

I said, "No, I've never had the pleasure." (Out of respect, I went along with her.)

She said, pointing to the empty chair beside me, "Well, let me introduce you."

As sure as I sit here today, I know he was right there with her during her final hours, to welcome her to the other side. Hours later, Suzette passed peacefully, and I am comfortable in my belief that her father was with her.

It is not uncommon in my profession to work with a hospice client whose spouse has recently died. There is often a familiar "presence" in the house after the first partner dies that is lasting evidence of their union. Tangible treasures include family photos, ashes, clothing never discarded, and projects that will not reach completion. But the strangest phenomena I experience include flickering lights, unusual reflections in mirrors, feeling a spiritlike presence, comforting aromas, objects often moved out of place, and pictures askew. Although most people would find these events unsettling, I often feel comforted, knowing that loved ones are "checking in" and awaiting a reunion with their beloved. I am learning lessons with every patient, every client I sit with, knowing as sure as I shake their hand in our first meeting that I am there to help them to die comfortably. We don't have all the answers in life, but there are some patterns of dying that cannot be ignored. I think we can all agree that although some things cannot be fully explained, that doesn't mean that there's no explanation; it's just beyond us.

Joani's Memory of Suzette

I am comforted every time I hear a story like Joani's because it teaches me that life goes by fast, but death happens like lightning. Life in comparison is long, and death is quick, so focus on life, make it good. Because even though death can be sad and painful, it's sadder and more painful to think that people squandered their life worried about what others think of them more than what they think of themselves. Live well, be there for your friends and family, be proud to be who you are, and remember that just because something feels hard to do for another, that doesn't mean you shouldn't do it. It was hard for me to sit with Shari, it hurt to hold her, and it was even harder to say good-bye, but I was there out of love and she knew it. Love is about sacrifice, and I promise that the sacrifices that you make for another will not only be worth every tear that you shed, they will one day be made *for* you instead of *by* you.

CHAPTER 7

The Hard Questions

I am often asked what happens to people who commit suicide. I want to dispel some myths that surround suicide, the most damaging being that people who commit suicide go to "hell." I also want to touch on religion and touch on the interpretation of the Bible. I get so many letters from people who think their son or daughter has gone to a bad place for committing suicide. So I will give you not only my perspective but the perspective of a priest who is also a medium.

People often ask me about reincarnation, so I want to say, for the record, that I don't know the answers around reincarnation. What I do know is that people on the other side remain available for me to communicate with as long as there is someone alive with whom they have an emotional connection. I do believe that reincarnation is entirely possible. People seem to be eerily drawn to a specific place and time in history, as if they'd been there before. But on this, I am not an expert. I personally have tried to focus on the here and now in life and not reach back to possible past lives. I believe in making the present a priority, and I try to live well and be happy. There are many wonderful authors who have researched reincarnation, and I encourage people to search for the answers they need in life. If reincarnation is important to you, then by all means, find your truth.

Because of my work and because of the show, people also seek me out to better understand the passing of someone who has been murdered.

Murder

I want to shed some light on what happens to people who pass at the hands of others. People who die at the hands of a killer carry a distinct energy, different from that of people who die in natural ways or in suicide or accidents.

It's important for families to understand that people who are murdered do not roam the earth unsettled. The deceased join family and friends who've already passed—the same family and friends who were not permitted by a bigger plan to intervene on behalf of the victim. There are circumstances where the death of one person would serve to change many lives through inspiring change for the better and serves as a powerful, positive rippling effect that moves more people than could be moved by the living. On the flip side, there are also occasions when a person's life plan included their being saved, when it was not in their "grand plan" to leave just yet. Although it seems greatly unfair sometimes, the living don't always see all the ways that a tragedy can invoke inspiration into a life. For instance, the child who was my first missing person's case was a stranger to me. Through looking for her, I learned about the child abduction alert system, Amber Alert, which was, at the time, very new. I came home from that case and set my sight on making Arizona a part of this valuable and necessary alert system. Once our system was up and running, it immediately saved many children's lives in Arizona. Without the child from my first case, who had died tragically, it may have taken Arizona much longer to create a statewide alert. Eventually, it would have happened, but which of the first saved would have fallen without the alert? In this way, the little victim saved other children from meeting a similar death. I will again remind you that we don't always see the many reasons to have faith in a "bigger plan." Sometimes we only see glimpses of the greater purpose, but those glimpses are only one small part of the plan. Those glimpses are most visible when held up against dark times for contrast. So when people wonder why bad things happen, I always believe that with good comes bad, but what we make of the bad is up to us.

The biggest tragedy is when people fail to change a life

for the better. It's never too late to decide to share your special gifts. These are the gifts that can only be found deep within the recesses of who you are. Sometimes a tragedy serves to call out these gifts lodged deep within us.

The deceased feel the pain of the living people whom they love, and they try to support them with their presence. Victims also serve as a reminder to the person who took their life. Not only is the deceased victim a reminder, but the living family members who lost a part of their future through the death of a loved one serve as reminders. I'm always moved when I see a family member of a victim on television talking to the parole board, telling them why the person who murdered his or her loved one should never come out of prison. My stance on murder is that if you willingly take an innocent life, you forfeit yours. I think the victim's family, who have to reach into their own pockets to pay to travel to stand before a parole board, are more important than the perpetrator. Hopefully, one day, there will be reform that will ease the lives of the victims and their families rather than the lives of the people who created the pain in the first place. We innately fight for those we love. The families of victims fight not only for the deceased but to remind everyone that the one they lost should matter to all. They're right for thinking so.

Families of victims will still be serving their sentence long after the perpetrator's ends. I want to help the families that deal with that kind of pain. I find a particular visual exercise helpful in processing the pain around loss. One such exercise is to lie on your bed and visualize a person you feel connected to who has passed away. Visualize the person standing at the foot of your bed holding a basket. Look at the detail of the basket and follow upward slowly with your eyes to the person's face. He or she is smiling and is backed by a white light. The person is capable of removing your pain and your worries. You're going to reach forward and place your problems in the basket. You can add as many as you want because the deceased has the ability to take all you have and gladly will do so. I once personally visualized my dad holding the basket. He was beaming light through his grin, and every hair was in place. I took my biggest problem at the time, which was a man whom I trusted but who turned out to not be so nice. I said, "Are you sure, Dad?"

He laughed and nodded his head. "Yes."

So I visualized the man himself being placed into the big basket feet first, until all you could see was the balding top of his head and his eyes peering angrily over the top of the basket. I've got to tell you, this is a great exercise. That helped me so much and allowed me to have a good laugh with my dad. My dad winked at me, turned, and carried away my troubles. Whenever I need him to take away my spiritual junk for me, I repeat the exercise. Anything that causes your heart to be heavy is worth placing in the basket. This exercise is also fantastic in strengthening the bond between yourself and those who've passed. They remain to help the ones they love, and even more so, they love to be needed still. So no worries about burdening the ones we love. They only feel burdened by their unfulfilled desire to be needed. So give them what they need, connection to us.

Another great exercise for people with a heavy heart is to visualize your heart filled with a magnificent white light. I've heard from healers that green is the heart chakra, which is great too. I like white, it works for me, like it's blowing away the painful rocks and cobwebs that can fill a heart. Like opening a window to a room that sometimes can feel cold and dark. I let in white because it reminds me of the spectacular white background that surrounds our loved ones when they appear from the other side. I always say, do what works for you! Green, white, whatever radiance you decide to introduce to your heart will be an improvement. Visualize the light until it not only fills every wall of your heart, but also spills over in all directions like a star. You can do this with your stomach if it's in knots or any part of your body that ails you.

You can also ask your deceased loved one to please add back to your heart what you feel was taken from you when he or she died. Close your eyes, take a deep breath, and allow the deceased to reinvest part of themselves back into your heart. It's a very uplifting exercise that also can be physically felt. Be sure to fully open your heart and mind to receive them back into your heart. Don't confuse desperation with openness. It's important to take a really big breath in through your nose and exhale through your mouth so that you can hear the air passing through. A quiet room is a big help for this exercise. This breathing puts you on the same energetic "page" as your deceased loved ones. They want to help. Let them remove your guilt/pain and replace it with their love.

As a footnote, victims who died are aware of everything that awaits the person who took their life. But that aside, spirits are more concerned with their loved ones than with the perpetrator. Families of victims often wonder what the deceased can see. They can see everything that awaits us, and when our lives are affected by the murderer, as they always are in a homicide, then the deceased care about the perpetrator only because the crime affects their own family and those they love. Victims care that a killer not be allowed to victimize another person, and they care about their own family. Other than that, the killer is unimportant to the deceased now.

On the flip side of death, people who have passed, even when they have been murdered, are aware of every emotion that the family feels, and they look for even the smallest joys over things like new puppies and celebrations. They want us to remember them and still love them, but they want us to move beyond our pain and experience joy again. Remember, they are there for each and every moment of happiness that you find or create. They love hearing us tell stories about them and watching us put up pictures of them at their zenith around the house—the portrait taken the day they were married; the WWII picture that they held onto with pride, the soldier looking handsome in his uniform; pictures of a mother who used to resemble a young Elizabeth Taylor, as she held her baby so close to her face with adoration; pictures of a father dancing with his daughter on her wedding day, the same little girl who wrapped her tiny infant hand around her daddy's finger years ago and stole his heart, which he'd never get back. Those pictures are the galleries of their life, the pictures that captured images of their existence, the ones that told the story of all they ever dreamt of having or being.

Those we love put thoughts into our heads, trying to prod us to join them in a walk down memory lane, or they talk us into making their favorite snack, which they loved but we never saw the value of until they died. Now it seems familiar and wonderful, even lovable! Isn't that just the way life works? Grandpa's deviled ham sandwiches with pickle relish on wheat bread that smelled so strong we held our noses every time he'd eat it has now become something that we crave ourselves. Whether for emotional comfort, or changing taste buds, we crave it. There are so many things to savor in life; it's sometimes hard to choose. Many families of murder victims feel guilty about being joyful, and they are sometimes too devastated to continue the experience of their loved one's life. I want to assure you that it is okay to move toward happiness. It's what preserves and protects the word *love.* And, yes, sometimes Grandpa's sandwich can remind us how much we love him.

Those who pass on insist on being remembered as they were when things were happy and untainted. They don't like their death to define their life. They are well loved and highly protected and often connecting with others who passed in a similar way. They also help support the living families of other victims who are now their friends. I find this predominantly the case with murders. It seems to be because most natural deaths don't usually cause people to reach out to strangers for support. Once the victim's family has reached out to another victim's family, the victims on the other side are brought together because two families who were previously strangers have now emotionally adopted each other. They have a common goal to help others. Also, the families tend to mention their new friends' loved one who was victimized almost in concert with their loved one, forming a deep bond.

I witnessed this bonding when I was a guest speaker for a grief counseling group that dealt with the topic of murder. Just talking to the members and seeing how they are there for each other was inspiring. On top of that, to see that they willingly experience the pain contained in the other members, as well as their own pain, made me sit back and fully feel this connection. At a time in a person's life when you would think the wounds are so severe that recovery would be impossible, I watched those people put their own grief aside to comfort another. I can honestly say, I have witnessed the best that a person is capable of being. When they had nothing left inside, they still reached into the depths of their soul and found strength for another in need.

Not all of us can say that about ourselves, but as long as we are willing to try, we take a step closer to becoming someone's lifeline. Which is really a gift that you will one day get back.

Addressing a killer's bad acts is important. I find it necessary to let people know that as bad as the killer's act was, it can no longer affect the person who died, who is now completely surrounded by immeasurable love and strength. He or she can never be touched again by anything bad, ever. This is important to express to the families of murder victims because their pain is so much deeper than in other types of losses. To lose a loved one at the hands of a person who had such hate and disregard for life resurrects images that are disturbing to the living, and far more scarring than other deaths. And for those of you who have been lucky enough never to be touched by murder, reach out to those who don't have the luxury of saying that. Even if all you can do is listen to them when they feel life has brought them to their knees, your kindness will help them to stand again. More important, this is for those who have been touched by murder: I hope you can look through my eyes, to know that the ones taken from you were surrounded with the arms of unbreakable love as soon as they crossed.

My heart and prayers go out to all the families of murder victims. Remember that every day forward is a day closer to your reunion with the ones who await you.

Suicide

Suicide is a way that few can understand. For the record, when a person commits suicide, he or she does not "go to hell." I know that religion has shared a different opinion on suicide; I am just sharing with you what I've seen myself. People who commit suicide are often good people who have a good heart. They also happen to be people who have a biological, chemical imbalance. We are not held responsible by the higher power for what we cannot help.

I often bring through people who have committed suicide, and they do express regret. They also express undying love and concern for their family and friends. They show me their childhood and what made them happy. They tell me how excited they are about their loved ones' lives since their passing. The babies born, the vibrant birthday parties, well-deserved graduations, blissful holidays, and visits they've made to their loved ones from the other side all are important to them. There are endless instances, but you get the idea. The living and dead are forever connected through our emotions and a continual attachment to one another that sees no reason to let go but every reason to hold on. Also, the deceased often acknowledge the people in the family who have passed away after them, and they convey the presence of the "newer" members that they now stand with to bring comfort to the living family members and friends, so that you know they're reunited with those who've more recently passed away. This is a communication that most deceased find important to mention to the living, letting them know that they are acting as a sort of host to those who have died more recently. It makes sense, since the deceased mostly remain to comfort the living, so of course they will ease minds and hearts by making their presence with the newly departed known to their living family. They often come through asking for forgiveness from the living and apologize for any pain they've caused. They often explain that if in life they had had the clarity they now have, they wouldn't have been suicidal. They seem to express their own grief over the loss of their life. At the same time they seem very happy to be healthy and to feel better than they ever could have imagined.

When I hear certain Christmas songs, my heart swells with love and pride in reflection of not only elegant words but the captivating sentiment being expressed. I'm not physically touching anything, but I'm moved by the words. When we die, all of the personality traits and preferences that we had in life move with us, but the feelings that seem to have the most strength in remaining present with the living are the experiences and emotions that caused us to feel good. It almost feels as though those moments prompted our soul to expand and deepen. So when our body no longer remains, the energy and depth we have inside breaks free and becomes even more awe-inspiring than before. Our limitations are removed and our real power, which was inside all along, can connect to anything, as well as gain for us a great sense of understanding. It seems as though the little traits stay with us. For instance, I'm a redhead, and all my life people have pointed out that redheads are feisty. Well, this may be true, but above that, I find being a redhead is part of who I am. So when I die, I expect that I will probably appear with red hair even if I die with gray, because it's a signature of who I am. We're all made up of these traits that affect how we feel inside or how we react in life. Some people have a great sense of humor. Often I bring them through telling jokes, because it's a part of who they are. Physical limitations die; our true selves live as we never could before and expand in our new form.

For the people left behind who lost a loved one to suicide, know this: you were loved by the person who died. Don't think that you're not loved and that maybe if the person loved you more, he or she wouldn't have committed suicide. It's not true. Those who died were not thinking straight, and they hurt as they observe the devastation they left behind. They often share with me in readings that they crave to hear that you know they love you and that they were overtaken by their inner imbalance. They don't think rationally about the person who has to find their body or the people who plan their funeral and cry for them. They only know they feel like they can't live in their body because it hurts, and they just want their inner suffering to stop. Anyone touched by a suicide will understand what I mean. For those who haven't had the experience, I can only say that some people feel such anguish inside that it feels like they're giving it everything they have just to stay another day. The solution of ending the bad feelings within them seems obvious to them. They see no other way. It's almost as if you had your emergency brake on in your car. You're driving with it fully pulled. Not only does driving feel difficult, but other things inside the car are breaking down because of that difficulty. Eventually, the car will break down.

Sometimes people who commit suicide are unstoppable, and survivors shouldn't beat themselves up thinking that somehow they could have prevented the passing. Many depressed or imbalanced people hide how they feel from those around them until it's too late. This is not to excuse the pain they cause, only to explain how they were feeling when they took their life. Often they feel undeserving of the love people have for them and see the living as better off without them. We know suicidal people are deserving of our love, but often they irrationally don't believe us. We all like to think that everyone else thinks and feels the way we do, but that's not the case. We're all different combinations of energy and often see things very differently from the people we stand next to. I think we've often listened to a person explain why he or she is justified in making a choice that others don't agree with, but as you look into the person's eyes, he or she truly doesn't see it the way you do. People are who they are; they may defy who we are, but we still can't change them, no matter how much we might want to.

People who survive those who commit suicide are often

left with abandonment issues. If that is your situation, please hear this: you are without question worth living for.

You lost someone who couldn't continue. When you feel low and it hurts, remind yourself that you are worth living for. You lost someone who you love who was unreachable when living, but without a doubt, that person is still with you, now balanced and able to understand you completely.

Since they've shed the physical ailment that was driving them, suicides have also lost feelings that they don't have control of themselves. Once the body is gone, they discover a clearer way of thinking and an even clearer ability to connect with others.

You carry an inner strength they didn't feel they had. From what I've seen and learned through readings from people who've committed suicide, their stories have some similarities. Their imbalance started out as mild depression early in youth. As they got older, it became harder to suppress and hide from others. Often they looked for a way to suppress their up-and-down tides of depression and resentment through alcohol or drugs. Some outgrew the level of medication they were prescribed to control their irrational highs and lows but didn't realize that the medication itself had become part of the problem. Some chemically imbalanced people just weren't heard by those whom they talked to about their problematic feelings. Not because the people didn't care, but because it can sometimes be hard to tell if someone is experiencing a chemical imbalance or feeling overwrought from having a really bad day.

Although they found it necessary to leave this life, they want you to continue your life and to be happy, because they love you. They'll walk through your life with you, grateful just to be a part of you. Remember, you're the part of them that gave them the glimmers of happiness in life. You'll see that eventually. Live your life without regret and "feel" their presence. They are now balanced, and they are your biggest cheerleader.

I want to stress that prevention of suicide is possible for some. Many depressed people are treatable by a physician or therapist who can help them achieve some clarity. The yellow pages have listings of suicide hotlines for most cities. There are many resources waiting to help.

I also want to remind people who are judgmental of families who have lost a loved one to suicide or who condemn the deceased to remember that people who commit suicide are human and deserve compassion and understanding. They shouldn't be seen as weak or shameful; rather, they were born with a combination of physical and emotional baggage that brought about their demise. We do have free will, but the other variables must also be considered. When I bring through a person who has recently passed from suicide, their energy to me feels like confusion or scattered energy. Their energy stabilizes over the first year after their passing. It's an energy adjustment that takes place within their soul, lending to a balance of their energy that they didn't have in life. They still have family around them, like any other person passed does. They have memories, love, and messages. They are not incomplete people. It was simply in their energy from birth to be challenged on many levels.

Some people may not understand this. Most people have experienced depression on one level or another and can relate to a feeling of grief and being misunderstood. People who are suicidal feel grief inside that consumes them; the pain feels to them as if someone died. Anyone who's loved and lost knows how deeply that hurts. The difference is it's everything within them that they feel die little by little, until they feel like a shell of a person. So to them they're already gone; suicide is a way of making it official.

If you see any signs that someone you love is depressed, reach out to him or her. Don't just say, "Hey, everything will be fine!" because the person is not hearing you. If there are chemical imbalances in the family, you might acknowledge this and share what you know with the person you're concerned about: "We come by this feeling naturally. It wouldn't hurt to go to the doctor and check this out together."

In some families, big noses are common; in others, green eyes. Some families have chemical imbalances; the condition is usually treatable. All we can do in life is reach out and try to meet people on familiar terms, and if it's not enough, at least you did *something*. All you can do is try. And remember, there is something greater than all of us that has a hand in death. You are not solely responsible for protecting a person from his or her genetics or own decisions. I see people carry a burden that somehow they should have been able to "fix" the person who committed suicide. Unfortunately, love and tears are not always enough to keep a person here. You did your best, and the person loves you for it, remember that.

Compassion for the families who have lost their loved one to suicide is key. I've talked to families who've been cast out of churches, shunned by their friends, and treated with contempt. How do you punish people who had no control over what the victims did to themselves? They'd give anything to have them back, and the person who committed suicide has paid the ultimate price. So when you're presented with an opportunity to be there for someone who's walked this path, be a good person and lend a shoulder.

I had an interesting experience after I wrote this section. I had dinner with a Catholic priest—who's a *medium*. A chance to ask all the questions I've ever had about being a medium who also believes in God. As I sat with him I thought, The idea that a priest could also be a medium goes against everything I've had to fight.

I asked him, "How do you balance your collar with being a medium? How do you balance what you teach with what you know inside to be true?"

He explained to me that there is interpretation in reading the Bible and he finds that his beliefs line up most of the time with what is written in the Bible.

I looked at him and I said, "People who commit suicide don't go to hell." (Did I just say that out loud? Me and my big mouth.)

I sat back and waited for him to show anger toward me. He leaned forward and said, "I know, I see them too. I counsel both the living and the dead."

My head was spinning as I tried to wrap my mind around this one. "So does that mean you're not going to call me the Antichrist?" I laughed.

"Not unless I'd apply that same term to myself," he said.

He and I spent a few moments studying each other, and both of us had a bit of a smirk.

I stared at the chain around his neck that existed only to hold a precious cross. His eyes were cool and contemplative. He almost seemed relieved to have another person like him to talk to. I had so many questions to ask him. This was an opportunity that most mediums never have, to speak to a priest who understands what it is to be a medium. He shared a story from his childhood that included parochial school and a nun who seemed to understand his path. He had questioned her about animals that die and his belief that they were in heaven.

She responded, and I paraphrase, "If we love animals, then God loves them too, so why wouldn't they go to heaven?" The father explained to me that this form of belief is called "theology from below," meaning common sense of the faithful people. I found this all terribly interesting and enlightening. I think that was a good answer from the sister, an honest, gentle response for a child.

We talked about many things that night, and he had questions for me, as I did for him. He wanted to know why sometimes the deceased appear in our head and sometimes they appear in front of us. I responded, "It has nothing to do with the medium. It seems to have everything to do with the deceased. It depends on how much energy the spirit has to come through with. This is usually determined by the life the person lived. If people knew how to connect to others emotionally in life, that carries over in their spirit and allows them to still reach the living easily as they did when alive. If people were isolated or didn't care for others in life, then that too carries over, and they will have a difficult time communicating still. It takes spirits far less energy to appear in our head than before our eyes. People who really had fun, dramatic, loving energy come through with more ease than someone who was confused, had troubled connecting with others emotionally, and didn't communicate well. It doesn't mean that one was bad, it's just an energy issue, and a question of whether they have the ability to express their energy well enough to reach the living.

"Father, you say that you know suicides cross over too. You don't believe that God would punish people with chemical imbalances as though they were in control of their actions, do you?" I'm aware that although this was in the form of a question, it was more of a statement.

He said, "No, I know they go to a good place to be with

their family and friends. I see them. Sometimes they seek me out. God knows chemically imbalanced people are people trying to deal with their own pain and they sometimes act in haste."

He went on to tell me that the church no longer takes the stance that those who commit suicide go to hell. The church allows that people who commit suicide are people not in control of themselves, so God wouldn't punish them. I don't know if this information is widely known. People still seem to think that those who commit suicide aren't heaven-bound. It's good to know that they are looked at by the church with understanding.

We talked about the church's feeling about mediums. I asked him, "Weren't we created in God's image?"

"Yes, Allison, we all were."

"Didn't Jesus appear to people after his death?"

"Yes, Allison, and King David appeared to a woman who summoned him after his death. It's in the Bible. This also testifies to the fact that life after death is possible. Not only to exist after your body dies, but for the living to communicate with those who've passed away. Allison, I'm sold on the fact that we're eternal.

"And Allison, the Church acknowledges that mystics truly exist, but the Church worries about evil spirits being able to be brought through by mediums. That's a concern."

"Father, I've never brought through anyone who's hurt anyone after death, have you?"

"No."

"Father, I witness evil more in the living than in those who are on the other side. For instance, when I'm at a murder trial, sitting within feet of evil, I often see the defendant sit there with a smile on his or her face while people testify how they witnessed the defendant carry out a killing. I'm more worried and shaken by them than I am by any spirit."

As our conversation continued, the father and I agreed that all babies are born in the image of God, but as we get older, we can find darkness within ourselves that we either embrace or try to change for the better.

I also wanted to ask him about the term "false prophets." "Father, does the church mean people who *pretend* to predict or *pretend* to commune with the dead?"

"Yes, people who don't actually have these abilities and are pretending to be a mystic not to help people but to harm them."

I'm glad I cleared that up, because it means that the church doesn't view mediums or mystics as bad. It means people who aren't what they claim to be are "false."

I can't begin to tell you how much I enjoyed meeting and breaking bread with such a rare man of the cloth. Then I wondered, Is he really so rare? I bet there are many people of God who can communicate with those who've passed on. I decided that yes, he is rare, because he's willing to understand and own both his priesthood and his mediumship abilities.

As I took in the enormity of this validation, I thought, I will never forget tonight, and it's true that anybody can be cut from the medium cloth. Anybody at all—a mother, a beggar, a child, a priest, *anyone.*

Because it's human and natural to connect with people we love, even after their physical body dies, their spirit remains and is stronger and clearer than ever. I realize I am just trying to learn all I can about life and living. It is comforting to me to know that throughout the Bible there are mentions of spirits appearing before the living and communicating. It's also comforting to know that there were many mediums who came before me, and there will definitely be many who come after me. I already know of three little girls in particular who will follow in my footsteps!

As I left the restaurant, saying good-bye to the father, I turned to my friend who had joined us and told her how blown away I was. In fact, it was she who had introduced us. I thanked her for an experience that I will continue to learn from the rest of my life.

Recently I was watching Larry King. He had a rabbi on who had negative energy, a man of the cloth, no less. Anyway, he was on the show arguing against three mediums who were also guests on the show, talking about life and death. Callers had glowing things to say about the mediums, who'd read them, and how they'd had a life-changing, uplifting experience through their readings. The skeptics smirked and ridiculed the callers. One even tried to "cold read" a caller (ask certain ambiguous questions that supposedly let anyone appear to read a person) but failed miserably at it, as the caller pointed out. One of the mediums then read the caller and demonstrated immediate results, and the caller was happy with his reading. So I sat back and observed this angry exchange of energy, and I thought, As far as religion goes, how is it so different when a medium asks to be believed, in that we can see something that may not be visible to all others? When you hold our reality next to that of a man of religion who's asking people to believe in a God that can't be seen? It's not so different. Both claims center around one's belief and personal spiritual experiences. Both are leaps of faith.

I believe in God, I believe I'm being taught many lessons in my life, and I'm paying attention to learn all that I can while I'm here. I'm not minimizing anyone's religion. I'm just drawing an obvious comparison of the two faiths. Often the faiths overlap, as they should, because both focus on something bigger than the living.

Being a compassionate person and embracing people when it's not the easiest thing to do or the most convenient time to do it are tests of character. If this chapter opens one mind and heart, then it has succeeded in changing a life for the better. What we learn in life and teach others is all a part of the domino effect. Differences are good, and keep in mind: as long as nobody's being hurt, to each his own.

And remember, as the father said, "We are eternal."

A Little Wiser

While preparing to write my final chapter of this book, I searched my soul for the words that could convey to my readers what I've learned in the year that's followed the debut of *Medium* and my first book, *Don't Kiss Them Good-Bye.*

I shook many hands in 2005, read many letters about loss, and placed myself in too many others' shoes to count. I was almost "blinded by the light" this year, excuse the humor, but I cling to it. Before becoming so public, I had successfully read many people, dismissed many skeptics, and asked the question so many of us ask every day, "Why me?"

Recently my friend Rich asked, "Allison, what do you want to do with your life?"

I hadn't been asked that in a long time, so I pondered the question. I responded, "Rich, I guess I want to help put away some more bad guys."

Rich looked at me with a look of friendship and sadness stirred together. "No, Allison, what do you want to do with your life that makes you happy?"

Wow! I don't think anyone had ever asked me that before. I have spent so much time being consumed by deep topics like murder and death that I didn't know that I was permitted another option. I thought, Well, my girls and Joe make me happy. If I have a lifetime with them, and my kids are healthy and passionate about life, then that sounds like a utopia to me.

I'm sharing this because, until Rich asked me that simple yet poignant question, I hadn't been outside the box that holds who I am inside it—the box of expectations and appearances, responsibility, and becoming set in one's ways. So I'm asking the same question of all my readers, "What are you going to do with your life that makes you happy?"

To answer this question, you must peek in every corner of your soul, look under every solid element of who you are. All it really takes is to do what most people do every day—analyze their past deeds that led them to where they are today. Except instead of beating yourself up for walking the road that led to who you became, look at who you *can* be. Some of you will say you have become who you set out to be, others will have to think long and hard about who that was that you dreamed of being.

When I was small, I wanted to grow up to help put bad guys away and make the world safer for kids. Check, I've done that, not on the scale I wanted to, but I am only one person. One, I've come to realize, is a great number. Even when you acknowledge that as one person you can't end world hunger by yourself or doctor everyone in the world, you still must know that you mattered to someone. Mattering to one person in life still changes the world through a domino effect. I love making others happy, and now I'm going to spend the next year finding out not only how to not apologize for who I am, but how to not let the problems of the world get me down. I'm going to concentrate on shaking more hands and hugging my kids.

On January 3, 2005, *Medium* first aired, and I lost my anonymity and opened myself up to a world of interesting, enlightened people, as well as some people who are constructed of anger and criticism. Patricia Arquette gave me some sound advice, "Don't read what the critics write. It can consume you."

Although, I must admit, I do love looking back at some of the TV critics' write-ups before the debut of *Medium*. Most were encouraging and wonderful, but I remember a couple that were along the lines of, and I paraphrase, "You don't have to be psychic to know this show will not last a season." I laugh when I read that one. These are the same critics who scoffed when I said that Patricia would be nominated for an Emmy Award, so what do they really know? They're people like anyone else, and I've come to realize that. You have to have a sense of humor in life and not become hardened by others. Humor will prolong your life and save you from becoming a callous individual.

When you feel empty inside or consumed by anger and think that you have all the answers to the world's problems, you become hardened. Although I feel very strongly about what I believe, I'm not trying to convert anyone. I share my experiences and hope they strike a chord with the people who feel that this example might be right for them. For those who haven't had my experiences, I try to be understanding. For those who condemn what I do, I try to be tolerant, knowing that I feel sorry for them in many ways. Everyone's born with a certain complex energy that will evolve as they get older, as long as they allow it to. There are those who've been on a soapbox so long they don't even hear whom they're talking at anymore. I say this because I've talked to many people who've had a moving reading that truly touched them, given either by myself or another medium, and they go home to have their spouse, friend, whoever ruin this special experience for them with snide remarks. It's necessary for me to point out to people that you can't let someone else's beliefs overshadow or carry more importance than your own. If someone you care about feels alleviated of a burden thanks to a reading, why would you or anyone want to negate that feeling? What could possibly motivate the spouse or friend who then steps in and deliberately hurts the person they're supposed to love?

When a person does this to you, you really need to look

at whether this person is thinking about you or simply react-
ing from his or her own fear and anxiety. If you're lucky
enough to have a great reading, don't let anyone steal your
thunder.

When you contemplate what makes you happy in life
and what will make your life feel well lived, remember this:
thinking about something is only the first step. You must
take action. Don't wait for someone to come along and hope
the person brings a big bag of happiness. Go get your own.

Last year I was given the opportunity to observe people
from around the world. I noticed a common thread connecting all of them. I traveled to Australia and New Zealand
for a book tour. It was beautiful, and the people were
friendly as well as comfortable with themselves, which was
nice to see. I visited Sydney, Melbourne, Auckland, and
Christchurch, and each city was special in its own way. Sydney was breathtaking with its Opera House and, let's not
forget, Pancakes on the Rocks, which has yummy food. It's
definitely a city that must be visited at least once. I will be
returning, and I will make sure that this time I get to visit the
magical carnival on the pier that at night lights up and looks
straight out of a child's dream, junk food and all. Melbourne
was memorable, where I met the Sisters in Crime when I
was a speaker at their memorable meeting of female crime
authors, forensic scientists, and such. Auckland was my
first stop. It has a small-town charm, and the people were
very kind. Christchurch had great Belgian suds and was
picturesque to boot.

When you travel, you will always notice some local differences, such as the food or the style of clothing. The most valuable part of my trip, though, was that I learned firsthand that people who have lost someone are the same no matter where they live. They feel pain, they need support from others, and each individual will deal with the pain the best he or she can, one way or another. I was met with some very enlightened faces who know their loved ones remain. They need no convincing because in their heart they already know that those who've died live again, just in a different form. They reside in a place of peace and faith. On the flip side, I had a skeptic stand up at a book signing, and I thought that my fans were going to lynch him, but I took care of that on my own with my words and soaked up their kind applause. Again, you have to learn to roll.

While I was writing this book, my husband, Joe, reminded me of a time when we were in our hotel room in New Zealand watching TV. We saw a commercial advertising a blanket. A man being interviewed about the blanket said, "Well, I was skeptical at first . . ."

Joe and I cracked up, because if there are people in the world who are skeptical of a blanket's performance, then truly anything in the world is capable of drawing skeptics. You have to take other people's opinions of what you do with a grain of salt. So the next time you're down on yourself about someone's criticism of *you,* remember that whether it be a man whose fiancée's family is skeptical of his ability to a good husband, or a sixteen-year-old girl who has people doubting her ability to graduate from high school, *everyone* is open to skepticism in life. Apparently, even inanimate objects aren't safe from criticism! Once you understand that, everyone in the world can work on letting it go and being happy, if for no other reason than because you deserve to be happy.

Don't be a person with a smile on your face and a sob on the inside. Be happy from the inside out. Consider that not every little exchange of energy in life, good or bad, is all up to you. We're all part of a bigger picture, and part of that picture is learning to release the burdens that we collected along the way in life. There will always be people who share my beliefs and others who will criticize both who I am and what I do. Guess what? It's okay. It's all a part of life. People question you so that you question yourself and deeply search your soul to find the answers within you that all add up to and equal you. And I'm not only talking about people who are skeptical about other people. I'm talking about people who are skeptical about religion, science, humanity, whatever. I realize they're necessary, because both action and reaction can show force, and force moves things, or else nothing would change.

So as I travel and meet people, I see why I have to keep being who I am. I have to because I too bring change in the world, as does every person who breathes. When you ignore who you are in order to please others or make them more comfortable, you deny your true energy and keep it from the world, replacing it with the stale ideas of people who are afraid to act and react and to participate in their own dynamic life force. I think that getting to the bottom of who we are can take a lifetime. That is truly the most challenging and rewarding puzzle of all. Skeptics aside, what really matters here is learning to stand tall in life and, when life calls for it, to kneel.

You better believe I pray. I recommend it. Sometimes it's what you need to carry you through an impossible time. Life is a series of choices. The more hands you shake in life, the more people you connect with, the more you learn about others and yourself. Everyone has something to teach and everyone has something to learn.

I've had an amazing year, never to be forgotten. I'm going to start my list of things to do next year, including taking my girls to SeaWorld for a family vacation. Also, I'm going to take my hubby, Joe, to Maui for some R and R and, although I think I'm already a pretty good friend, I'm going work on spending more time with my friends. So, what would you add to your own list to make sure you live well, to make sure that life doesn't pass you by? Because it's never too late to make it count.

After a busy yet spectacular year, I've watched my family's life change. Joe has taken up golf and loves it and is jokingly called "Mr. Medium" by his friends. He's retired early to support the girls and me. He wants to be there for us when we need him.

My oldest daughter is every bit like her character on the show. She's the sixth-grade class representative, an honors math student, and the youngest girl on the Junior High Cheer Line, yikes!

My middle daughter, whom I lovingly call my "centered" daughter (Get it? I know, bad joke), is in the third grade. She also very much the same as the character on *Medium.* She's my quirky one, and she can be heard in her school choir singing louder than all the other kids. You gotta love her. She marches to the beat of her own drummer.

My youngest daughter, my baby, who was born on the Fourth of July, is in the first grade now. She's taking ice-skating lessons, which she loves, Brownies too! And she still has me wrapped around her little finger. So although their mom has a show based on her life, writes books, and traipses through the desert in hiking boots looking for the missing, my girls still think I'm just another overbearing mom who they know loves them more than anything.

To all of you who've sent me letters asking about my family and sending me cards thanking me for writing my books, I hope I've answered your questions. Thank you for taking the time to write me, to read my books, and to watch *Medium.* Although it has been an incredible year, I hope to spend each year making other people's lives a little easier and becoming a little bit wiser.

ACKNOWLEDGMENTS

I want to acknowledge my editor, Nancy Hancock; my publicist, Ellen Silberman; and the rest of the team at Simon & Schuster for standing behind my books and inviting me into their family. Glenn Caron for his passion in writing. Patricia Arquette for capturing me and sharing my story. And Paramount and NBC for continuing a show that enlightens many. A special thank you to Drew Gomez and John Pagoto at Dilemma.

Last, but certainly not least, I want to thank the people who are mentioned and whose stories are shared in this book. Please know we are all connected and those who've moved on are never gone from you.

About the Author

Allison DuBois's unique story, the inspiration of the hit NBC TV show *Medium,* started during her final semester at an Arizona university, while she was an intern at the district attorney's office. Soon after, researchers at the university documented her ability through a series of tests in which she scored exceptionally high on accuracy and specificity. This validation bolstered Allison's confidence in her decision to become a professional medium and profiler instead of a prosecuting attorney.

In her short career, Allison has conducted over two thousand personal readings. In those readings, she helps to ease the pain people feel from losing a loved one. She had spent four years participating in various tests for the university.

Allison donates her time to missing and murdered persons and criminal cases for agencies across the country. She is contacted by law enforcement agencies and families to help find missing and murdered people. Allison also assists in jury selection for district attorneys' offices. Each of these activities is a means for her to give back to the world for being so blessed.

Allison maintains close ties to the show *Medium* as a consultant.

Allison has been featured on *The Today Show, The Big Idea with Donny Deutsch,* and *Last Call with Carson Daly,* and in countless magazines and newspapers.